THE CAT

BEING A RECORD OF THE ENDEARMENTS AND
INVECTIVES LAVISHED BY MANY WRITERS
UPON AN ANIMAL MUCH LOVED
AND MUCH ABHORRED

COLLECTED, TRANSLATED AND ARRANGED BY

AGNES REPPLIER

AUTHOR OF "THE FIRESIDE SPHINX"

WITH ILLUSTRATIONS BY
ELISABETH F. BONSALL

You hold your race traditions fast,
While others toil, you simply live;
And, based upon a stable past,
Remain a sound conservative.

New York
STURGIS & WALTON
COMPANY
1912

TABLE OF CONTENTS

THE CAT AMONG FRIENDS

CONTENTS

THE CAT AMONG FOES

THE CAT LOVER SPEAKS

CAT PORTRAITS

CONTENTS

CONTENTS

THE CAT IN THE NURSERY

ACKNOWLEDGMENTS

My sincere thanks are due to all the authors who have courteously permitted me to include their work in this volume, which otherwise would have been hopelessly inadequate. Also to Mr. Marriott Watson, who has allowed me to reprint Mrs. Marriott Watson's two admirable poems, and to Mrs. Charles Dudley Warner, who has given me the extract from Mr. Warner's "Calvin." Also to Harper and Brothers, publishers of Mr. Swinburne's poems and of Mr. Janvier's stories; to The Macmillan Company, publishers of Mr. Matthew Arnold's letters and poems; to D. Appleton and Company, publishers of Mr. Huxley's life and letters; to the Houghton Mifflin Company, publishers of Mr. Warner's "Calvin, a Study of Character"; to Mr. John Lane, publisher of Mr. Benson's and of Mrs. Marriott Watson's poems; to Charles Scribner's Sons, publishers of Mr. Herford's poems; and to Mr. William Heinemann, publisher of Margaret Benson's "The Soul of a Cat."

THE CAT

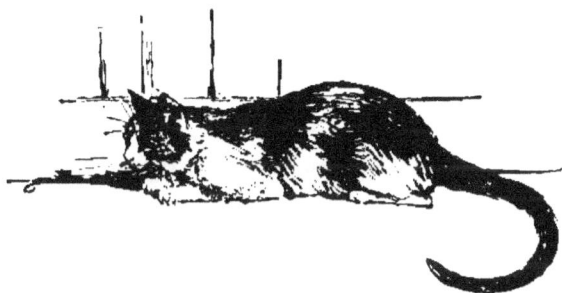

INTRODUCTION

It is not the easy and grateful task to trace the cat, as we may trace the dog, through history and literature. All nations have conspired to praise the animal which loves and serves. Few and cold are the praises given to the animal which seldom loves and never serves, which has only the grace of companionship to offer in place of the dog's passionate fidelity. There is no cat to put by the side of the hound, Argos,—Argos, old, blind, shivering on a dung-heap, who recognizes Odysseus in his beggar's garb, and dies of joy at his master's return. There is no such epitaph on a cat as that of Simonides on a hound of Thessaly:

"Surely even as thou liest in this tomb, I deem the wild beasts yet fear thy white bones, Lycas; and thy valour great Pelion knows, and the lonely peaks of Cithæron."

There is no word of Shakespeare's to which the cat-lover may turn with delight, as the hunter turns to the gallant lines of Theseus:

" My hounds are bred out of the Spartan kind,
So flew'd, so sanded; and their heads are hung
With ears that sweep away the morning dew."

As a matter of fact, all the earliest notices of the cat are peevish outcries against her freebooting instincts, her spirit of stubborn independence. She was centuries winning a foothold in society even as the

" harmless necessary cat,"

that rid the household of mice, and any deviation from duty's path brought down upon her graceful head a torrent of abuse.

" These vylanous false cattes
Were made for mice and rattes,
And not for byrdes small,"

writes John Skelton, with unwarranted confidence in the discrimination of nature's laws.

" Grimalkin, the foul Fiend's cat,
Grimalkin, the witche's brat,"

runs an old rhyme, expressing the popular prejudice of its day.

"A ha-penny cat may look at a king,"
says a Scotch proverb, blatantly contemptuous of
Pussy's place in the order of creation.

It was not until the arts of peace had supplanted
the arts of war, and men had leisure to make themselves comfortable, that the cat emerged from obscurity, and evinced a laudable disposition to share
this comfort. It was not until a growing taste for
luxury softened the old hardy, turbulent life, that
the cat felt herself at ease by the firesides of civilization. She was cautious in her advances, sharing
the deep mistrust which she inspired, and reserved
even with her friends. The most domestic of animals, by virtue of her attachment to her home, she
has never made a full surrender of her freedom.
The most companionable of animals, by virtue of
her softness, her silence, her orderly instincts and
her innate self-respect, she grants her friendship
only on terms of equality. The most suave of animals, she remains a mystery, as impenetrable now
as when she shared the witch's knowledge and the
witch's doom.

For all these reasons, people who write about
cats do so, for the most part, in terms of exaggera-
tion. The world is divided into men and women
who love cats, and men and women who cordially
detest them. It seems difficult to preserve an atti-

tude of neutrality towards a beast whose most striking characteristic is indifference. This is especially the case ·with French authors. From the shuddering cry of Ronsard,

> " No living man, of things beneath the sky,
> Can hate a cat more bitterly than I;
> I hate its eyes, its face, its very stare;"

to the fervent lines of Baudelaire, whose love for his cats was a fantastic passion, we find much that is beautiful, but little that is temperate. " Only a Frenchman," observes M. Gautier, " can understand the subtle organization of a cat." Only a Frenchman can write about his cats in minute detail, with delicate sympathy, and with a high quality of imagination. The Germans have been prompt to recognize Pussy's mysterious personality, and keenly alive to her domestic usefulness; but they have seldom sought to make of her a friend.

In England and in America the cat's progress to favour has been slow and sure. A hundred years lie between Miss Joanna Baillie's

> —" careful, comely, mousing cat,"

and Mr. Swinburne's

> " Stately, kindly, lordly friend,"

and, in these hundred years, English writers have at last learned to value at their utmost worth the qualities which so long repelled enthusiasm. They have much to say about the cat's beauty; but they grow eloquent over her love of liberty, her manifest reserves, her contemptuous serenity of bearing. They describe with delight her nocturnal wanderings, her human interest in her own comfort, the calmness with which she permits herself to be waited upon, and her steadfast refusal to bend her will to the capricious demands of humanity. They have discovered that she is the most charming of play-fellows, the most soothing of companions; and that the friendship which is hard to win and hard to hold is worth at least as much as the friendship which is given for the asking.

I have laboured *con amore* to pursue the vicissitudes and the triumphs of the cat, as set forth in French and English letters. I have tracked her soft footprints along quiet paths and broad high- . ways. I offer the fruits of my toil to all who share my deference for the most self-respecting, my admiration for the most charming, my love for the most lovable of beasts.

The Cat Among Friends

A cat I keep,
That plays about my house,
Grown fat with eating
Many a miching mouse.

Herrick

THE CAT

The Cat

On some grave business, soft and slow,
Along the garden-paths you go,
    With bold and burning eyes:
Or stand, with twitching tail, to mark
What starts and rustles in the dark,
    Among the peonies.

The dusty cockchafer that springs
Upon the dusk with whirring wings,
    The beetle, glossy-horned,
The rabbit pattering through the fern,
May frisk unheeded, by your stern
    Preoccupation scorned.

You go, and when the morning dawns
O'er blowing trees and dewy lawns,
    Dim-veiled with gossamer,
When cheery birds are on the wing,
You creep, a wild and wicked thing,
    With stained and starting fur.

You all day long, beside the fire,
Retrace in dreams your dark desire,
    And mournfully complain

3

In grave displeasure, if I raise
Your languid form to pet or praise;
    And so to sleep again.

The gentler hound that near me lies,
Looks up with true and tender eyes,
    And waits my generous mirth;
You do not woo me, but demand
A gift from my unwilling hand,
    A tribute to your worth.

You loved me when the fire was warm,
But, now I stretch a fondling arm,
    You eye me and depart.
Cold eyes, sleek skin, and velvet paws,
You win my indolent applause,
    You do not win my heart.

                    ARTHUR CHRISTOPHER BENSON.

The Cat of Egypt

THE number of domestic animals in Egypt is very great, and would be still greater, were it not for what befalls the cats. As the females, when they have kittened, no longer seek the company of the males, these last, to obtain once more their companionship, practise a curious artifice. They seize the kittens, carry them off, and kill them; but do not eat them afterwards. Upon this, the females, being deprived of their young, and longing to supply their place, seek the males once more, since they are particularly fond of their offspring.

On every occasion of a fire in Egypt, the strangest prodigy occurs with the cats. The inhabitants allow the fire to rage as it pleases, while they stand about at intervals and watch these animals, which, slipping by the men, or else leaping over them, rush headlong into the flames. When this happens, the Egyptians are in deep affliction. If a cat dies in a private house by a natural death, all the inmates of the house shave their eyebrows. The dead cats are taken to the city of Bubastis, where they are embalmed, after which they are buried in certain sacred repositories.

HERODOTUS.

Version of George Rawlinson, M.A.

Montaigne and his Cat

WHEN my cat and I entertain each other with mutual antics, as playing with a garter, who knows but that I make more sport for her than she makes for me? Shall I conclude her to be simple that has her time to begin or to refuse to play, as freely as I have mine. Nay, who knows but that it is a defect of my not understanding her language (for doubtless cats can talk and reason with one another) that we agree no better; and who knows but that she pities me for being no wiser than to play with her; and laughs, and censures my folly in making sport for her, when we two play together.

MONTAIGNE.

The Cat as a Royal Envoy

THENNE the kynge of the beastis saide to the catte: "Syr Tybert, ye shal now goo to Reynart, and saye to hym this seconde tyme that he come to court, for to answere unto the plea; for though he be felle to other beastis, he trusteth you wel, and shal doo by your counseyl. And telle hym if he come not, he shal have the thirde warning, and if he thenne come not, we shal procede by ryght agenste hym, and alle hys lyneage wythout mercy."

The catte spake: "My lord the kynge, they that thus counseylde you were not my frendes. What shal I doo there? Reynart wyl not for me neyther come ne abyde. I beseeche you, dere kynge, sende some other to hym. I am a catte, lytyl and feeble. Bruyn the beare, which was so grete and strong, coude not brynge hym. How shold I thenne take it on honde?"

"Nay," said the kynge, "Sir Tybert, ye ben wyse and wel lerned. Though ye be not grete, many do more wyth crafte and connyng than with myght and strengthe."

Thenne said the catte: "Syth it muste nedes be don, I muste take it upon me. God give grace that I may wel achieve it, for my hearte is heavy and evil willed thereto."

Reynard the Fox. From the edition printed by Caxton in 1481.

The Lover Whose Mistresse Feared a Mouse

The Squirrel thinking nought,
   That feately cracks the nut,
The greedie Goshawke wanting prey,
   In dread of Death doth put;
But scorning all these kindes,
   I would become a Cat,
To combat with the creeping Mouse,
   And scratch the screeking Rat.

I would be present, aye,
   And at my Ladie's call,
To gard her from the fearfull Mouse,
   In Parlour and in Hall;
In Kitchen, for his Lyfe,
   He should not shew his hed;
The Pease in Poke should lie untoucht
   When shee were gone to Bed.

The Mouse should stand in Feare,
   So should the squeaking Rat;
All this would I doe if I were
   Converted to a Cat.

GEORGE TUBERVILLE.

8

THE CAT

An Appreciation

I VALUE in the cat the independent and almost ungrateful spirit which prevents her from attaching herself to any one, the indifference with which she passes from the salon to the housetop. When we caress her, she stretches herself and arches her back responsively; but this is because she feels an agreeable sensation, not because she takes a silly satisfaction, like the dog, in faithfully loving a thankless master. The cat lives alone, has no need of society, obeys only when she pleases, pretends to sleep that she may see the more clearly, and scratches everything on which she can lay her paw."

CHATEAUBRIAND *to M. de Marcellus.*

The Contemplative Life

FROM the dawn of creation the cat has known his place, and he has kept it, practically untamed and unspoiled by man. He has *retenue*. Of all animals, he alone attains to the Contemplative Life. He regards the wheel of existence from without, like the Buddha. There is no pretence of sympathy about the cat. He lives alone, aloft, sublime, in a wise passiveness. He is excessively proud; and, when he is made the subject of conversation, will cast one glance of scorn, and leave the room in which personalities are bandied. All expressions of emotion he scouts as frivolous and insincere, except, indeed, in the ambrosial night, when, free from the society of mankind, he pours forth his soul in strains of unpremeditated art. The paltry pay and paltry praise of humanity he despises, like Edgar Poe. He does not exhibit the pageant of his bleeding heart; he does not howl when people die, nor explode in cries of delight when his master returns from a journey. With quiet courtesy, he remains in his proper and comfortable place, only venturing into view when something he approves of, such as fish or game, makes its appearance. On the rights of property he is firm. If a strange cat enters his domain, he is up in claws to resist invasion. It was for these qualities, probably, that the cat was worshipped by the ancient Egyptians.   ANDREW LANG.

The Cat

I like the simple dignity
   That hedges round the cat;
You never see her showing off,
   She lets the dog do that.

You never catch her leaping hoops,
   Nor prancing on the floor
Upon two legs, when generous
   Dame Nature gave her four.

We train the dog to hunt the birds,
   And beat him when he fails.
He works all day, and never gets
   A single taste of quails.

The cat is wiser far than he,
   She hunts for birds to eat;
She does not run her legs off, just
   To give some man a treat.

All cats, no matter what their breed,
   Are born aristocrats;
They never, like the terriers, make
   A trade of killing rats.

The cat will rid the house of rats,
   Because she likes the fun,
No man can say she's moved to it,
   Because he wants it done.

11

Man harnesses the lightning, and
   Makes steam perform his will,
The horse and dog his bond-slaves are,
   The cat eludes him still.

The dog's man's servant, plaything, drudge,
   A foolish altruist;
The cat, in spite of man, remains
   Serene, an egotist.

Talk not to me about your dog,
   It is but idle chat;
Give me that calm philosopher
   Of hearth and home, the cat.

                RUTH KIMBALL GARDINER.

THE CAT ═══════════════

Around, in sympathetic mirth,
  Its tricks the kitten tries;
The cricket chirrups on the hearth,
  The crackling fagot flies.

             OLIVER GOLDSMITH.

Firelight

Musing, I sit on my cushioned settle,
   Facing the firelight's fitful shine;
Sings on the hob the simmering kettle,
   Songs that seem echoes of " auld lang syne."

And close beside me the cat sits purring,
   Warming her paws at the cheery gleam;
The flames keep flitting, and flicking, and whirring,—
   My mind is lapped in a realm of dream.

HEINRICH HEINE,
Translated by Sir Theodore Martin.

A Poet's Kitten

I HAVE a kitten, my dear, the drollest of all creatures that ever wore a cat's skin. Her gambols are incredible, and not to be described. She tumbles head over heels several times together. She lays her cheek to the ground, and humps her back at you with an air of most supreme disdain. From this posture she rises to dance on her hind feet, an exercise which she performs with all the grace imaginable; and she closes these various exhibitions with a loud smack of her lips, which, for want of greater propriety of expression, we call spitting. But, though all cats spit, no cat ever produced such a sound as she does. In point of size, she is likely to be a kitten always, being extremely small for her age; but time, that spoils all things, will, I suppose, make her also a cat. You will see her, I hope, before that melancholy period shall arrive; for no wisdom that she may gain by experience and reflection hereafter will compensate for the loss of her present hilarity. She is dressed in a tortoise-shell suit, and I know that you will delight in her.

WILLIAM COWPER *to Lady Hesketh.*

The Kitten

Wanton droll, whose harmless play
Beguiles the rustic's closing day,
When, drawn the evening fire about,
Sit aged Crone and thoughtless Lout,
And child upon his three-foot stool,
Waiting till his supper cool;
And maid whose cheek outblooms the rose,
As bright the blazing faggot glows,
Who, bending to the friendly light,
Plies her task with busy sleight;
Come, shew thy tricks and sportive graces,
Thus circled round with merry faces.

Backward coiled, and crouching low,
With glaring eyeballs watch thy foe;
The housewife's spindle whirling round,
Or thread or straw, that on the ground
Its shadow throws, by urchin sly
Held out to lure thy roving eye.
Then, onward stealing, fiercely spring
Upon the futile, faithless thing.
Now, wheeling round with bootless skill,
Thy bo-peep tail provokes thee still,
And oft, beyond thy curving side,
Its jetty tip is seen to glide;
Till, from thy centre starting far,
Thou sidelong rear'st, with tail in air

THE CAT

Erected stiff, and gait awry,
Like Madam in her tantrums high;
Though ne'er a Madam of them all
Whose silken kirtle sweeps the hall,
More varied trick and whim displays,
To catch the admiring stranger's gaze.
Doth power in measured verses dwell,
All thy vagaries wild to tell?
Ah no! the start, the jet, the bound,
The giddy scamper round and round,
With leap, and jerk, and high curvet,
And many a whirling somerset
(Permitted be the modern Muse
Expression technical to use),
These mock the deftliest rhymester's skill,
So poor in art, though rich in will.

The nimblest tumbler, stage-bedight,
To thee is but a clumsy wight,
Who every limb and sinew strains
To do what costs thee little pains,
For which, I trow, the gaping crowd
Requites him oft with plaudits loud.
But, stopped the while thy wanton play,
Applauses too *thy* feats repay:
For then, beneath some urchin's hand,
With modest pride thou takest thy stand,
While many a stroke of fondness glides
Along thy back and tabby sides.

17

Dilated swells thy glossy fur,
And loudly sings thy busy purr,
As, timing well the equal sound,
Thy clutching feet bepat the ground,
And all their harmless claws disclose,
Like prickles of an early rose;
While softly from thy whiskered cheek
Thy half-closed eyes peer mild and meek.

Whence hast thou then, thou witless Puss,
The magic power to charm us thus?
Is it, that in thy glaring eye
And rapid movements we descry,
While we at ease, secure from ill,
The chimney corner snugly fill,
A lion darting on his prey?
A tiger at his ruthless play?
Or is it that in thee we trace,
With all thy varied wanton grace,
An emblem, viewed with kindred eye,
Of tricksy, restless infancy?
Ah! many a lightly-sportive child,
Who hath, like thee, our wits beguiled,
To dull and sober manhood grown,
With strange recoil our hearts disown.
Even so, poor kit! must thou endure,
When thou becomest a cat demure,
Full many a cuff and angry word,
Chid roughly from the tempting board.

THE CAT

And yet, for that thou hast, I ween,
So oft our favoured playmate been,
Soft be the change which thou shalt prove,
When time hath spoiled thee of our love;
Still be thou deemed, by housewife fat,
A comely, careful, mousing cat,
Whose dish is, for the public good,
Replenished oft with savoury food.
Nor, when thy span of life be past,
Be thou to pond or dunghill cast;
But gently borne on good man's spade,
Beneath the decent sod be laid,
And children show with glistening eyes,
The place where poor old Pussy lies.

JOANNA BAILLIE.

19

The Kitten

A KITTEN is the joy of a household. All day long this incomparable actor plays his little comedy, and those who search for perpetual motion can do no better than watch his antics. His theatre is always open, any room suffices him for a stage, and he has need of few accessories. A scrap of paper, a bit of string, a spool, a pen, these are enough to incite him to marvellous acrobatic feats. "Everything that moves," says Moncrif, "serves to interest and amuse a cat. He is convinced that nature is busying herself with his diversion; he can conceive of no other purpose in the universe; and when we sport with him, and make him leap and tumble, he probably takes us for pantomimists and buffoons."

Even when a kitten is quiet, he is the drollest of creatures. What a spice of innocent malice in his half-shut eyes! His head, heavy with sleep, his outstretched paws, his air of ineffable languor, all tell of comfort and content. A little drowsing cat is an image of perfect beatitude. Look at his ears. How big and comical they are. No sound, however faint, escapes them. Look at his eyes when he opens them wide. How quick and keen their glance. Who is that knocking? Who is that crossing the room? What is there good to eat in box, or bundle, or basket? The ruling passion of a kitten is curiosity, and in this regard he is uncommonly like a child. "When a cat enters a room for the first time," says Rousseau in "Emile," "he prowls into every corner, he cannot rest until he has made himself familiar with his surroundings. So does a young child behave when he is beginning to walk and talk. So does he question the unknown world he is entering."

There is no more intrepid explorer than a kitten. He makes perilous voyages into cellar and attic, he scales the roofs of neighbouring houses, he thrusts his little inquiring nose into half-shut doors, he lays up for future use a store of useful observation, he gets himself into every kind of trouble, and is always sorry when it is too late. It is amazing to see a kitten climb a tree. Up he goes from bough to bough, higher and higher, as though bent on enjoying the view from the top. He does not ask where this delightful adventure is taking him. He pays no heed to the diminishing size of the branches, and it is only when they sway beneath his weight that he realizes the impossibility of mounting any further. Then fear gripes his heart, and he mews appealingly for help. Somebody must hasten with a ladder to his rescue;

and, until aid comes, he slides pitifully and peril-
ously along an upper branch, clawing it with
desperate precautions. His heart, we know, is
beating as though it would break, his agility has
deserted him, his audacity has given way to despair.

Les Chats, JULES HUSSON CHAMPFLEURY.

Good and Bad Kittens

Kittens, you are very little,
  And your kitten bones are brittle,
If you'd grow to Cats respected,
  See your play be not neglected.

Smite the Sudden Spool, and spring
  Upon the Swift Elusive String;
Thus you learn to catch the wary
  Mister Mouse, or Miss Canary.

That is how, in Foreign Places,
  Fluffy Cubs with Kitten faces,
Where the mango waves sedately,
  Grow to Lions large and stately.

But the Kittencats who snatch
  Rudely for their food, or scratch,
Grow to Tomcats gaunt and gory,
  Theirs is quite another story.

Cats like these are put away
  By the dread S. P. C. A.,
Or to trusting Aunts and Sisters
  Sold as Sable Muffs and Wristers.

OLIVER HERFORD.

23

Yet can thy humble roof maintaine a quire
    Of singing crickets by thy fire;
And the brisk mouse may feast herselfe with crumbs,
    Till that the green-eyed kitling comes.

                          ROBERT HERRICK.

Dido

WE have got the prettiest kitten you ever saw, — a dark tabby,— and we have christened her by the heathenish name of Dido. You would be very much diverted to see her hunt Herbert all round the kitchen, playing with his little bare feet, which she just pricks at every pat; and the faster he moves back, the more she paws them, at which he cries, "Naughty Dido!" and points to his feet, and says, "Hurt, hurt, naughty Dido!" Presently he feeds her with comfits, which Dido plays with awhile, but soon returns to her old game.

ROBERT SOUTHEY *to Lieutenant Southey.*

In Memoriam

ALAS, Grosvenor, this day died poor old Rumpel, after as long and happy a life as cat could wish for, if cats form wishes on that subject. His full titles were: —

" The most Noble the Archduke Rumpelstiltz-chen, Marquis Macbum, Earl Tomlemagne, Baron Raticide, Waowhler, and Skaratch."

There should be a court mourning in Catland, and if the Dragon [1] wear a black ribbon round his neck, or a band of crape, *a la militaire*, on one of his fore legs, it will be but a becoming mark of respect.

As we have no catacombs here, he is to be decently interred in the orchard, and catmint planted on his grave. Poor creature, it is well that he has thus come to his end, since he had grown to be an object of pity. I believe we are, each and all, servants included, more sorry for his loss, or rather more affected by it, than any one of us would like to confess.

I should not have written to you at present, had it not been to notify you of this event.

ROBERT SOUTHEY *to Grosvenor C. Bedford.*

[1] Bedford's cat.

The Strength Which Lies in Delicacy

THE cat's energy is subdued into an exquisite
moderation. Other animals roughly employ what
strength they happen to possess, without reference
to the smallness of the occasion; but the cat uses
only the necessary force. One day I watched a
kitten playing with a daffodil. She sat on her
hind legs, and patted the flower with her paws,
first with the right paw, then with the left, making
the light yellow bell sway from side to side, yet
not injuring a petal or a stamen. She took delight, evidently, in the very delicacy of the exercise; whereas a dog or a horse has no enjoyment of
delicacy in its own movements, but acts strongly
when it is strong, without calculating whether the
energy used may not be in great part superfluous.
This proportioning of force to the need is an evidence of refinement in manners and in art. If
animals could speak, the dog would be a blunt,
blundering, outspoken, honest fellow; but the cat
would have the rare grace of never saying a word
too much.

PHILIP GILBERT HAMERTON.

The Companionable Cat

MY cat in winter time usually sleeps upon my dog, who submits in patience; and I have often found her on horseback in the stable, not from any taste for equestrianism, but simply because a horse-cloth is a perpetual warmer when there is a living horse beneath it.   She loves the dog and horse with the tender regard we have for foot-warmers and railway rugs during a journey in the depth of winter; nor have I ever been able to detect in her any worthier sentiment towards her master.   Yet of all animals that we can have in a room with us, the cat is the least disquieting.   Her presence is soothing to a student, as the presence of a quiet nurse is soothing to an invalid.   It is agreeable to feel that you are not absolutely alone, and it seems to you, when you are at work, as if the cat took care that all her movements should be noiseless, purely out of consideration for your comfort.   Then, if you have time to caress her, you know that she will purr a response, and why inquire too closely into the sincerity of her affection?

PHILIP GILBERT HAMERTON.

The Kitten and the Falling Leaves

That way look, my infant, lo!
What a pretty baby show!
See the kitten on the wall,
Sporting with the leaves that fall,
Withered leaves,— one — two — and three,—
From the lofty elder-tree!
Through the calm and frosty air
Of this morning bright and fair
Eddying round and round they sink,
Softly, slowly: one might think,
From the motions that are made,
Every little leaf convey'd
Sylph or fairy hither tending,—
To this lower world descending,
Each invisible and mute,
In his wavering parachute.

But the kitten, how she starts,
Crouches, stretches, paws, and darts!
First at one, and then its fellow,
Just as light and just as yellow;
There are many now,— now one,—
Now they stop, and there are none.
What intenseness of desire
In her upward eye of fire!
With a tiger-leap half way
Now she meets the coming prey,
Lets it go as fast, and then

29

Has it in her power again;
Now she works with three or four,
Like an Indian conjuror;
Quick as he in feats of art,
Far beyond in joy of heart.
Were her antics play'd in the eye
Of a thousand standers-by,
Clapping hands with shout and stare,
What would little Tabby care
For the plaudits of the crowd?
Over happy to be proud,
Over wealthy in the treasure
Of her own exceeding pleasure!

WILLIAM WORDSWORTH.

Pussy-Willows

I sometimes think the Pussy-Willows grey
Are Angel Kittens who have lost their way,
   And every Bulrush on the river bank
A Cat-Tail from some lovely Cat astray.

Sometimes I think perchance that Allah may,
When he created Cats, have thrown away
   The Tails he marred in making, and they grew
To Cat-Tails and to Pussy-Willows grey.

OLIVER HERFORD.

The London Cat

On summer mornings from four A. M. to five, London ceases to belong to the world of men, and is given over to birds and cats. At this really bewitching hour, for the city then is beautiful, the cats may be seen, as at no other time, *rerum domini*, masters of the town. It is not for nothing that the race has for generations maintained its independence, and asserted its right to roam. For at that hour all the dogs are shut up, all the boys and grown people are asleep. The city is theirs. The demeanour of London cats at four A. M. is one of assured freedom. They stroll about the streets and gardens with a quiet air of possession. They converse in the centre of highways. They walk with feline *abandon* and momentary magnificence over open squares. In the silver grey of a London dawn they are no longer domestic pets, they are gentlemen at large.

The Spectator.

THE CAT

Practice

Cultivate your garden, said Goethe and Voltaire,
Every other task is wasted and dead-born;
Narrow all your efforts to a given sphere,
Seek your Heaven daily in a bit of ground.

So my cat behaves.   Like a veteran,
He brushes well his coat before he sits to dine;
All his work is centred in his own domain,
Just to keep his spotless fur soft, and clean, and fine.

His tongue is sponge, and brush, and towel, and curry-
    comb,
Well he knows what work it can be made to do,
Poor little wash-rag, smaller than my thumb.

His nose touches his back, touches his hind paws too,
Every patch of fur is raked, and scraped, and
    smoothed;
What more has Goethe done, what more could Voltaire
    do?

From the French of Hippolyte Taine.

Auld Bawthren's Song

The gudewife birrs wi' the wheel a' day,
> Three threeds an' a thrum;
A walth o' wark, an' sma' time for play,
Wi' the lint sae white and worset grey
Work hard she maun, while sing I may,
> Three threeds an' a thrum.

The gudewife rises frae out her bed,
Wi' her cozy nicht-mutch round her head,
To steer the fire to a blaze sae red,
An' her feet I rub wi' welcome glad.

I daunder round her wi' blythesome birr,
An' rub on her legs my sleek warm fur;
Wi' sweeps o' my tail I welcome her,
An' round her rin, wherever she stir.

The men-folk's time for rest is sma',
They're out in the sunshine, an' out in the snaw,
Tho' cauld winds whistle, or rain should fa',
I, in the ingle, dae nought ava'.

I like the gudeman, but loe the wife,
Days mony they've seen o' leil and strife;
O' sorrow human hours are rife;
Their haud's been mine a' the days o' my life.

34

THE CAT

Auld Bawthren grey, she kitten'd me here,
An' wha was my sire I didna spier;
Brithers an' sisters smoor'd i' the weir,
Left me alane to my mither dear.

As I grew a cat wi' look sae douce,
She taught me to catch the pilf'rin mouse;
Wi' the thievish rottons I had nae truce,
But banished them a' frae the maister's house.

Mither got fushionless, auld, an' blin,
The bluid in her veins was cauld an' thin,
Her claws were blunt, an' she couldna rin,
An' t' her forbears was sune gathered in.

Now I sit hurklin' aye in the ase,
The queen I am o' that cozy place;
As wi' ilka paw I dicht my face,
I sing an' purr wi' mickle grace,
        Three threeds an' a thrum,
        Three threeds an' a thrum.

Anonymous.

To my Lord Buckhurst, Very Young, Playing with a Cat

The am'rous youth, whose tender breast
Was by his darling cat possest,
Obtain'd of Venus his desire,
Howe'er irregular his fire.
Nature the power of love obey'd,—
The cat became a blushing maid;
And, on the happy change, the boy
Employ'd his wonder and his joy.
Take care, O beauteous child, take care,
Lest thou prefer so rash a pray'r:
Nor vainly hope the Queen of Love
Will e'er thy fav'rite's charms improve.
Oh, quickly from her shrine retreat,
Or tremble for thy darling's fate.
The Queen of Love, who soon will see
Her own Adonis live in thee,
Will lightly her first loss deplore,
Will easily forgive the boar.
Her eyes with tears no more will flow,
With jealous rage her breast will glow,
And on her tabby rival's face
She deep will mark her new disgrace.

MATTHEW PRIOR.

A Cat

Philosopher and comrade, not for thee
The fond and foolish love which binds the dog;
Only a quiet sympathy which sees
Through all my faults, and bears with them awhile.
Be lenient still, and have some faith in me,
Gentlest of sceptics, sleepiest of friends.

JULES LEMAÎTRE *to his Cat.*

The Cat Among Foes

No
favour can
win gratitude from a cat

La Fontaine

To a Cat which had Killed a Bird

O cat in semblance, but in heart akin
To canine raveners, whose ways are sin,
Still at my hearth a guest thou dar'st to be?
Unwhipt of Justice, hast no dread of me?
Or deem'st the sly allurements shall avail
Of purring throat and undulating tail?
No! as to pacify Patroclus dead,
Twelve Trojans by Pelides' sentence bled,
So shall thy blood appease the feathery shade,
And for one guiltless life shall nine be paid.

AGATHIAS, *Translation of Richard Garnett.*

On a Cat, Killed as she was Robbing a Dove-Cote

Poor Puss is gone!— 'tis Fate's decree,
  Yet I must still her loss deplore;
For dearer than a child was she,
  And ne'er shall I behold her more.

With many a sad, presaging tear,
  This morn I saw her steal away,
While she slipped off without a fear,
  Except that she should miss her prey.

I saw her to the dove-house climb,
  With cautious feet and slow she stept,
Resolved to balance loss of time
  By eating faster than she crept.

Her subtle foes were on the watch,
  And marked her course, with fury fraught;
And while she hoped the birds to catch,
  An arrow's point the huntress caught.

In fancy she had slain them all,
  And drunk their blood and sucked their breath;
Alas! she only got a fall,
  And only drank the draught of death.

THE CAT

Why, why was pigeon's flesh so nice,
   That thoughtless cats should love it thus?
Hadst thou but lived on rats and mice,
   Thou hadst been living still, poor Puss!

Cursed be the taste, howe'er refined,
   That prompts us for such joys to wish;
And cursed the dainty, where we find
   Destruction lurking in the dish.

From the Arabic in IBN ALALAF ALNAHARWANY.

The Witch Cat

INNUMERABLE legends cluster around the cat during the picturesque centuries of superstition, when men were poor in letters, but rich in vivid imaginings; when they were densely ignorant, but never dull. Even after the Dark Ages had grown light, there was no lifting of the gloom which enveloped Pussy's pathway, there was no visible softening of her lot. The stories told of her impish wickedness have the same general character throughout Europe. We meet them with modest variations in France, Germany, Sweden, Denmark, England, Scotland and Wales. It was a belated woodcutter of Brittany who saw with horror-stricken eyes thirteen cats dancing in sacrilegious glee around a wayside crucifix. One he killed with his axe, and the other twelve disappeared in a trice. It was a charcoal-burner in the Black Forest who, hearing strange noises near his kiln at night, arose from bed, and stepped into the clearing. Before him, motionless in the moonlight, sat three cats. He stooped to pick up a stone, and the relic of Saint Gildas he carried in his bosom fell from its snapt string upon the ground. Immediately his arm hung helpless, and he could not touch the stone. Then one of the cats said to its companions: " For the sake of his wife, who is my gossip, sisters, let him go!" and the next morning he was found lying unconscious, but unharmed, across the forest road.

From Scandinavia, where the fair white cats of Freija were once as honoured as were Odin's ravens and Thor's goats, comes the tale of the haunted mill, in which dreadful revelry was heard at night, and which had been twice burned to the ground on Whitsun Eve. The third year, a travelling tailor, pious and brave, offered to keep watch. He chalked a circle on the floor, wrote the Lord's prayer around it, and waited with patience until midnight. Then a troop of cats crept stealthily in, carrying a great pot of pitch which they hung in the fireplace, lighting the logs beneath it. Soon the pitch bubbled and seethed, and the cats, swinging the pot, tried to overturn it. The tailor drove them away; and when one, who seemed to be the leader, sought to pull him gently outside the magic circle, he cut off its paw with his knife. Upon this, they all fled howling into the night; and the next morning the miller saw with joy his mill standing unharmed, and the great wheel turning merrily in the water. But the miller's wife was ill in bed; and, when the tailor bade her good-bye, she gave him her left hand, hiding beneath the bedclothes the right arm's bleeding stump.

45

There is also a Scandinavian version of the ever famous story which Sir Walter Scott told to Washington Irving, which "Monk" Lewis told to Shelley, and which, in one form or another, we find embodied in the folk-lore of every land,— the story of the traveller who saw within a ruined abbey a procession of cats, lowering into its grave a little coffin with a crown upon it. Filled with horror, he hastened from the spot; but when he reached his destination, he could not forbear relating to a friend the wonder he had seen. Scarcely had the tale been told, when his friend's cat, who lay curled up tranquilly by the fire, sprang to his feet, cried out, "Then I am the King of the Cats!" and disappeared in a flash up the chimney.

The Fireside Sphinx, AGNES REPPLIER.

Anathema Maranatha

That vengeaunce I aske and crye,
By way of exclamacyon,
On all the whole nacyon
Of cattes wylde and tame;
God send them sorowe and shame!
That cat especyally
That slew so cruelly
My lytell pretty sparowe,
That I brought up at Carowe.
  O cat of churlyshe kynde,
The Fynde was in thy minde
When thou my byrde untwynde!
I would thou haddest ben blynde!
The leopardes savage,
The lyons in theyr rage,
Myght catche thee in theyr pawes!
And gnawe thee in theyr jawes!
The serpentes of Lybany
Myght stynge thee venymously!
The dragones with theyr tonges
Myght poyson thy lyver and longes!
The mantycors of the montaynes
Myght fede them on thy braynes!
Melanchates, that hounde
That plucked Actæon to the grounde,
Gave hym his mortall wounde,

Chaunged to a dere,
The story doth appere,
Was chaunged to an harte:
So thou, foule cat that thou arte,
The selfesame hounde
Myght thee confounde,
That his owne lord bote,
Myght byte asondre thy throte!
  Of Inde the gredy grypes
Myght tere out all thy trypes!
Of Arcady the beares
Myght plucke awaye thyne eares!
The wylde wolfe Lycaon
Byte asondre thy backe bone!
Of Ethna the brennynge hyll,
That day and nyghte brenneth styl,
Set in thy tayle a blase,
That all the world may gase
And wonder upon thee!
From Ocyan the greate sea
Unto the Isles of Orchady;
From Tyllbery ferry
To the playne of Salysbery!
So trayterously my byrde to kyll,
That never wrought thee evyll wyll!

The Boke of Phylyp Sparowe, JOHN SKELTON.

48

False Gods

Now shall ye see in Babylon gods of silver, and
of gold, and of wood. . . . . Their faces are blacked
thorow the smoke that comes out of the temple. Upon
their bodies and heads sit battes, swallowes, and birds,
and the cats also. By this you may know that they
are no gods; therefore fear them not.

BARUCH, Apocrypha.

Ailurophobia

MY research brought to me indisputable evidence concerning the large number of people in whom the presence of a cat gives rise to a variety of symptoms. In such persons, the feeling caused by seeing a cat is instantaneous. In the asthma victims, it is slower and cumulative, and may not be felt at all for twenty minutes or more. Certain persons, on seeing a cat, have other symptoms, with or without oppression of breathing. There may be only fear, terror, disgust. There may be added chilly sensations, horripilation, weakness, locked jaw, or, as in one case, fixed open jaw, rigidity of arms, pallor, nausea, rarely vomiting, pronounced hysterical convulsions, and even temporary blindness. These pass away with removal of the cat, but in a few examples leave the sufferer nervously disturbed for a day. Two report themselves as apt to have dreams of cats, what one of them calls " cat mares."

Five persons, three being women, are alarmed in the presence of the greater cats, caged tigers or lions. A soldier of distinction, much given when younger to tiger hunting, is undisturbed by these great felines, but terrified by the tame cat.

On a study of those who, at sight of cats, have fear, horror, and, in varying degrees, emotional disturbances and distinct physical symptoms, and those whom unseen cats affect, we observe that the same symptomatic expressions attend both groups.

In the first set, sight of the cat informs. Then there are fear, horror, disgust, and more or less of the nervous symptoms already described. In the second set, those who are conscious of unseen cats, some sense, other than sight or hearing, gives the information, and then the symptoms are much the same as when the cat is seen.

S. Weir Mitchell, M.D.

51

Antipathy

MATHIOLUS tells us of a German who, coming in
winter time into an inn to sup with him and some
other of his friends, the woman of the house, being
acquainted with his temper (lest he should depart
at sight of a young cat which she kept to breed
up), had beforehand hid her kitling in a chest, in
the room where the company sat at supper. But
though the German had neither seen nor heard the
little animal, yet after some time that he had sucked
in the air infected by its breath, that quality of
his temperament which had antipathy unto cats
became sorely disturbed. He began to sweat, and
of a sudden to grow pale; and, to the wonder of
all who were present, he cried out in an anguished
voice that in some corner of the room there was a
cat lay hid.

Wonders of the Little World, 1678,
NATHANIEL WANLEY.

A Martyr

IN the Reigne of Queene Mary (at which time Popery was much exalted), then were the Round-heads — *i. e.*, the monks and friars — so odious to the people, that, in derision of them, was a Cat taken on a Sabbath day, with her head shorne as a Fryer's, and the likenesse of a vestment cast over her, with her feet tied together, and a round piece of paper like a singing Cake between them; and thus was she hanged on a gallows in Cheapside, neere to the Crosse, in the parish of Saint Mathew. Which Cat, being taken down, was carried to the Bishop of London, and by him sent to Doctor Pendleton (who was then preaching at Paul's Cross), commanding it to be shown to the Congregation. The Round-head Fryers cannot abide to heare of this Cat.

> *Twenty Lookes over all the Round-heads in the World*, 1648.

The Old Cat and the Young Mouse

A young Mouse, small and innocent,
Implored an old Cat's clemency:
" Raminagrobis, let me live!
Your royal mercy, monarch, give!
A Mouse so little, sir, as I
A tiny meal can ill supply.
How could I starve a family?
Host, hostess, only look at me.
I fatten on a grain of wheat,—
A mite my dinner makes complete;
I'm thin, too, now,— just wait a bit,
And for your children I'll be fit."
Thus spoke the little Mouse, aggrieved;
The old Cat answered: " You're deceived.
Go, tell the deaf and dumb,— not me,
Cats never pardon, so you'll see.
The law condemns, and you must die;
Descend, and tell the Fates that I
Have stopped your preaching, and be sure
My children's meals will be no fewer."
He kept his word; and to my fable
I add a moral, as I'm able:
Youth hopes to win all by address;
But age is ever pitiless.

JEAN DE LA FONTAINE.

THE CAT

A Cat's Conscience

A dog will often steal a bone,
But conscience lets him not alone,
And by his tail his guilt is known.

But cats consider theft a game,
And, howsoever you may blame,
Refuse the slightest sign of shame.

When food mysteriously goes,
The chances are that Pussy knows
More than she leads you to suppose.

And hence there is no need for you,
If Puss declines a meal or two,
To feel her pulse and make ado.

Anonymous.

Punchinello and the Cat

PUNCHINELLO lay on the floor in a corner of the nursery. His little master had gone to school, and deserted him.

The cat slipped in through a half-open door. She held in her mouth a ball of cotton which she had carried carefully upstairs, but which she dropped as soon as she caught sight of Punchinello. "What is that?" she asked herself uneasily, and proceeded to make a stealthy tour of the room, feigning indifference, but creeping ever closer and closer to the fantastic little figure on the floor. He lay quiet, but she was none the less suspicious of his intentions. Crouching and quivering, she glared at him through half-shut eyes, as though seeking to measure his strength before challenging him with the war-cry of her race.

— Ffff!

Punchinello, wholly unconcerned, never so much as winked.

A second and a louder challenge.

— Ffffffff!

Punchinello dozed tranquilly.

Then from the cat's little body came a sound, deep and terrible, like the rumbling of far-off thunder.

— Rrrrrrrrr!

There was no response. The cat's back rose into a miniature mountain, her fur bristled, all the grace and beauty which are born of a tranquil soul deserted her. She curveted sideways as though meditating an attack, and then sank slowly on the floor in the superb attitude of an Egyptian sphinx. Only her gleaming eyes and twitching tail betrayed the tumult of her soul. Like a diplomatist who, in his library, studies a map of Europe and plans the destruction of an empire, so the cat concealed her murderous designs until the time was ripe for action. She even seemed disposed to abandon the game of war, and leave her defenceless enemy at peace; but this was pure hypocrisy. Another moment, and she had leaped upon Punchinello, burying her claws in his breast, and rending into shreds his rich embroidered coat. Well she knew that his master was at school, and, heedless of all the care that had been lavished upon her education, she forgot that she was a domestic cat, and became a beast of prey.

Poor Punchinello! Of what avail now was his drum, or the stick with which he had dealt so many merry blows? The cat dragged him over the floor, flung him hither and thither, clawed off his wig (unspeakable indignity!), lacerated him with her

57

sharp claws, and tossed him high into the air. Then, as his body fell limply to the ground, she sat down upon him, quietly and gravely, less like a conqueror than like a judge who has sentenced a criminal, and who is unvexed by the dissenting opinions of the vulgar. Her fury subsided into calm, her green eyes opened unblinkingly upon the sun, she assumed once more her sphinx-like attitude, her air of impenetrable mystery.

After a few minutes spent in profound contemplation, the cat arose, stretched herself, and coldly and silently departed.

JULES HUSSON CHAMPFLEURY.

The Cat-Lover Speaks

You see the beauty of the world
Through eyes of unalloyed content,
And in my study chair upcurled,
Move me to pensive wonderment.

Le Chat Noir

Half loving-kindliness, and half disdain,
Thou comest to my call, serenely suave,
With humming speech and gracious gesture grave,
In salutation courtly and urbane.
Yet must I humble me thy grace to gain,
For wiles may win thee, but no arts enslave,
And nowhere gladly thou abidest, save
Where naught disturbs the concord of thy reign.

Sphinx of my quiet hearth! who deignst to dwell
Friend of my toil, companion of mine ease,
Thine is the lore of Ra and Rameses;
That men forget dost thou remember well,
Beholden still in blinking reveries,
With sombre, sea-green gaze inscrutable.

GRAHAM TOMSON.

The Cat's Progress

OUTLAWED for centuries, driven ruthlessly from hearth and home, then tolerated merely as a useful chattel, the cat has gradually insinuated herself into polite society. She has made herself at home in library and drawing-room, she has reserved for occasional use kitchen, dining-room and office. She may be seen drowsing for hours on the bed, she takes exclusive possession of the most comfortable armchair, she curls herself at will on her master's knee, and, when the frost deepens, she always monopolizes the warmest corner by the fire.

This is the progress, and these are the admitted triumphs of the cat. She has conquered and domesticated man, reduced him to the rôle of an obedient servant, and required of him that he shall provide her with the luxuries she loves. In doing this, he but performs his duty, and need expect no gratitude. The loud declarations of naturalists count for little by the side of such a candid confession as that of M. de Cherville, who tells us in one of his charming essays that for two years he has obsequiously served a little cat, born under his roof, and raised by his careful hands. For two years he has studied her tastes, and shown her every attention in his power; and never in all this time has he won from her the smallest token of regard. Never has she vouchsafed him a caress by way of thanks, nor consented to go to him, when called with loving words and tender cajoleries.

Here is a picture painted with sincerity, and in unvarnished colours. No devotion on our part can soften these little tyrants whom we never dream of resisting, and who end by triumphing even over the dog, their ancient and hereditary foe. Alas, poor dog! He is the perfect friend of man, the slave of our caprices, " mechanically faithful," to use an admirable phrase of Mme. de Custine, and, through no fault of his own, condemned to love us. Now he sees himself dispossessed, not only of our exclusive favour, but of his accustomed place in our chimney corner. Hardly has he stretched himself on the rug before the fire, when the cat, apparently on the best of terms with her old adversary, approaches silently and softly, like a skilled strategist, and seats herself by his side, as close as she can very well get to him. This done, she proceeds to roll herself into a ball, then rises and stretches her limbs, then turns round and round, so as to toast every part of her little body, always contriving to disturb the dog, and compel him to insensibly give place. The poor beast tucks his tail out of sight, then his paws and his nose; but finding himself still in the cat's way, and not knowing how to resist such subtle encroachments, he finally makes up his mind to leave the warm fire, and take refuge in some chillier corner of the room where he may sleep in peace.

Un Peintre de Chats, HENRY HAVARD.

THE CAT

Arsinoë's Cats

Arsinoë the fair, the amber-tressed,
    Is mine no more;
Cold as the unsunned snows are is her breast,
    And closed her door.
No more her ivory feet and tresses braided
    Make glad mine eyes;
Snapt are my viol strings, my flowers are faded,
    My love-lamp dies.

Yet, once, for dewy myrtle-buds and roses,
    All summer long,
We searched the twilight-haunted garden closes
    With jest and song.
Ay, all is over now,— my heart hath changéd
    Its heaven for hell;
And that ill chance which all our love estrangéd
    In this wise fell:

A little lion, small and dainty sweet,
    (For such there be!)
With sea-grey eyes and softly stepping feet,
    She prayed of me.
For this, through lands Egyptian far away,
    She bade me pass:
But, in an evil hour, I said her nay,
    And now, alas!

Far-travelled Nicias hath wooed and won
      Arsinoë,
With gifts of furry creatures, white and dun,
      From over sea.

GRAHAM TOMSON.

Free, and proud, and glad as they,
    Here to-day
Rests or roams their radiant child,
Vanquished not, but reconciled;
Free from curb of aught above
Save the lovely curb of love.

Love, through dreams of souls divine,
    Fain would shine
Round a dawn whose light and song
Then should right our mutual wrong,—
Speak, and seal the love-lit law,
Sweet Assisi's seer foresaw.

Dreams were theirs; yet haply may
    Dawn a day
When such friends and fellows born,
Seeing our earth as fair at morn,
May, for wiser love's sake, see
More of heaven's deep heart than we.

           ALGERNON CHARLES SWINBURNE.

Postscript to a Rondeau, Addressed by Mme. la Duchesse du Maine to her Favourite Cat

My pretty Puss, my solace and delight,
To celebrate thy loveliness aright
I ought to call to life the bard who sung
Of Lesbia's sparrow with so sweet a tongue;
But 'tis in vain to summon here to me
So famous a dead personage as he,
And you must take contentedly to-day
This poor rondeau that Cupid wafts your way.

Translated by EDMUND GOSSE.

Epitaph on the Favourite Cat of Mme. la Duchesse du Maine

Puss passer-by, within this simple tomb
  Lies one whose life fell Atropos hath shred;
The happiest cat on earth hath heard his doom,
  And sleeps forever in a marble bed.
Alas! what long delicious days I've seen!
  O cats of Egypt, my illustrious sires,
You who on altars, bound with garlands green,
  Have melted hearts and kindled fond desires,
Hymns in your praise were paid, and offerings too;
  But I'm not jealous of those rites divine;
Since Ludovisa loved me, fond and true,
  Your ancient glory was less proud than mine.
To live, a simple pussy, by her side,
  Was nobler far than to be deified.

  *Translated from the French of La Mothe le Vayer
    by* EDMUND GOSSE.

The Cat's Coronach

And art thou fallen, and lowly laid,
The housewife's boast, the cellar's aid,
    Great mouser of thy day!
Whose rolling eyes and aspect dread
Whole whiskered legions oft have fled
    In midnight battle fray.
There breathes no kitten of thy line
But would have given his life for thine.

. Oh, could I match the peerless strain
That wailed for black Sir Roderic slain,
    Or that, whose milder tone,
O'er Gertrude, fall'n in beauty's prime,
The grace of Pennsylvania's clime,
    Raised the sepulchral moan;
Such strain might burst th' eternal bar,
And reach thy spirit from afar.

But thou, remote from pain and strife,
Now reap'st the meed of virtuous life
    In some Elysian grove,
Where endless streams of milk abound,
And soft valerian paints the ground
    Thy joyous footsteps rove;
With Tasso's cat by poems named,
And Whittington's, in story famed,
    Requies cat in pace.   *Anonymous.*

72

Cat Portraits

A great Angora watched his collieship.
And, throned in monumental calm, surveyed
His effervescence, volatility, clamour on slight occasions,
Fussiness, herself immobile, imperturbable.

William Watson

THE CAT

The Cat of Great Britain

THE Cat is surely most like to the Leoparde, and hathe a great mouthe, and sharp teeth, and a long tongue, plyante, thin and subtle. He lappeth therewith when he drinketh, as other beastes do that have the nether lip shorter than the over; for, by cause of unevenness of lips, such beastes suck not in drinking, but lap and lick, as Aristotle saith, and Plinius also. He is a swifte and merye beaste in youthe, and leapeth, and riseth on all things that are tofore him, and is led by a straw, and playeth therewith; and he is a righte heavye beaste in age, and full sleepye, and lyeth slyly in waite for Mice, and is ware where they bene more by smell than by sighte, and hunteth, and riseth on them in privy places. And when he taketh a Mouse, he playeth therewith, and eateth him after the play. He is a cruell beaste when he is wilde, and dwelleth in woods, and hunteth there small beastes as conies and hares.

Translated from the Latin by Thomas Berthlet. Printed by Wynkyn de Worde. 1498.

Catus, the Cat

As to the Cat's Eyes, authors say that they shine in the Night, and see better at the full, and more dimly at the change of the Moon. Also that the Cat doth vary his Eyes with the Sun; the Pupil being round at Sunrise, narrow towards Noon, and not to be seen at all at Night, but the whole Eye shining in the darkness. These appearances of the Cat's Eyes I am sure are true; but whether they answer to the time of the Day, I have never observed. It is a crafty, subtle, watchful Creature, very loving and familiar with Mankind; but the mortal Enemy of the Rat, Mouse, and every sort of Bird, which it seizes on as its Prey. Its flesh is not generally eaten, yet in some Countries is esteemed an excellent dish.

The Compleat English Physician, 1693,

WILLIAM SALMON.

THE CAT

For whoso woldè senge a cattès skyn,
Thenne wolde the cat wel dwellen in hir in;
And if the cattès skyn be slyk and gay,
She wol nat dwelle in housè half a day.
But forth she wol, er any day be dawed,
To shewe hir skyn, and goon a-caterwawed.

CHAUCER.

Hinse of Hinsefeld

I HAVE added a romantic inmate to my family,
— a large bloodhound, allowed to be the finest dog
of the kind in Scotland, perfectly gentle, affectionate, good-natured, and the darling of all the
children. He is between the deer-greyhound and
mastiff, with a shaggy mane like a lion, and always
sits beside me at dinner, his head as high as the
back of my chair; yet it will gratify you to know
that a favourite cat keeps him in the greatest possible order, insists upon all rights of precedence,
and scratches with impunity the nose of an animal
who would make no bones of a wolf, and pulls down
a red deer without fear or difficulty. I heard my
friend set up some most piteous howls (and I assure
you the noise was no joke), all occasioned by his
fear of passing Puss, who had stationed himself on
the stairs.

SIR WALTER SCOTT *to Joanna Baillie.*

Hodge

I SHALL never forget the indulgence with which Dr. Johnson treated Hodge, his cat, for whom he himself used to go out and buy oysters, lest the servants, having that trouble, should take a dislike to the poor creature. I am unluckily one of those who have an antipathy to a cat, so that I am uneasy when I am in the room with one; and I own I frequently suffered a good deal from the presence of this same Hodge. I recollect him one day scrambling up Dr. Johnson's breast, apparently with much satisfaction, while my friend, smiling and half whistling, rubbed down his back, and pulled him by the tail; and when I observed he was a fine cat, saying, " Why, yes, sir, but I have had cats whom I liked better than this "; and then, as if perceiving Hodge to be out of countenance, adding, " but he is a very fine cat, a very fine cat indeed."

This reminds me of the ludicrous account which he gave Mr. Langton of the despicable state of a young gentleman of good family: " Sir, when I heard of him last, he was running about town, shooting cats." And then, in a sort of kindly reverie, he bethought himself of his own favourite cat, and said, " But Hodge shan't be shot; no, no, Hodge shall not be shot."

Life of Samuel Johnson, JAMES BOSWELL.

Hodge, the Cat

Burly and big his books among,
  Good Samuel Johnson sat,
With frowning brows and wig askew,
His snuff-strewn waistcoat far from new;
So stern and menacing his air,
  That neither " Black Sam " nor the maid
To knock or interrupt him dare;
  Yet close beside him, unafraid,
    Sat Hodge, the cat.

" This participle," the Doctor wrote,
  " The modern scholar cavils at,
But,"— even as he penned the word,
A soft protesting note was heard:
The Doctor fumbled with his pen,
  The dawning thought took wings and flew,
The sound repeated came again,
  It was a faint reminding " Mew! "
    From Hodge, the cat.

" Poor Pussy! " said the learned man,
  Giving the glossy fur a pat,
" It is your dinner time, I know,
And,— well, perhaps I ought to go;

80

THE CAT

For if Sam every day were sent
  Off from his work your fish to buy,
Why, men are men, he might resent,
  And starve or kick you on the sly;
    Eh! Hodge, my cat?"

The Dictionary was laid down,
    The Doctor tied his vast cravat,
And down the buzzing street he strode,
Taking an often-trodden road,
And halted at a well-known stall:
  "Fishmonger," spoke the Doctor gruff,
"Give me six oysters, that is all;
  Hodge knows when he has had enough,
    Hodge is my cat."

Then home; Puss dined, and while in sleep
    He chased a visionary rat,
His master sat him down again,
Rewrote his page, renibbed his pen;
Each i was dotted, each t was crossed,
  He laboured on for all to read,
Nor deemed that time was waste or lost
  Spent in supplying the small need
    Of Hodge, the cat.

The dear old Doctor! fierce of mien,
    Untidy, arbitrary, fat,
What gentle thoughts his name enfold!
So generous of his scanty gold,
So quick to love, so hot to scorn,
    Kind to all sufferers under heaven,
A tenderer despot ne'er was born;
    His big heart held a corner even
        For Hodge, the cat.

                    SUSAN COOLIDGE.

Atossa

I HAVE just been called to the door by the sweet voice of Toss, whose morning proceedings are wonderful. She sleeps — She has just jumped on my lap, and her beautiful tail has made this smudge, but I have put her down again. I was going to say that she sleeps on an armchair before the drawing-room fire; descends the moment she hears the servants about in the morning, and makes them let her out; comes back and enters Flu's room with Eliza regularly at half-past seven. Then she comes to my door, and gives a mew, and then,— especially if I let her in, and go on writing or reading without taking any notice of her,— there is a real demonstration of affection, such as never again occurs in the day. She purrs, she walks round and round me, she jumps in my lap, she turns to me and rubs her head and nose against my chin, she opens her mouth and raps her pretty white teeth against my pen. Then she leaps down, settles herself by the fire, and never shows any more affection all day.

MATTHEW ARNOLD *to his mother.*

Atossa

Thou hast seen Atossa sage
Sit for hours beside thy cage;
Thou wouldst chirp', thou foolish bird,
Flutter, chirp,— she never stirred!
What were now these toys to her?
Down she sank amid her fur;
Eyed thee with a soul resign'd,
And thou deemedst cats were kind!
Cruel, but composed and bland,
Dumb, inscrutable, and grand;
So Tiberius might have sat,
Had Tiberius been a cat.

Poor Matthias, MATTHEW ARNOLD.

Moumoutte Blanche

I HAD been long without a cat when Moumoutte Blanche was brought to me. She lay, a tiny ball of white fur, on the red carpet, and I lifted her up very gently with both hands, so that she might be reassured, and say to herself after the manner of kittens: " This is a man who understands how to hold me, who is a friend, and whose caresses I can venture to receive with condescension !" Such a pretty little cat as she was, her baby eyes yellow and gleaming, her tiny nose rose pink, her fur deep and soft, warm to the touch, and beautifully clean. A patch of black on her forehead looked like a coquettish little bonnet, another on her shoulders, like a cape; her tail was black, her throat and paws whiter than swan's down. She weighed nothing, this bundle of nerves, of snowy fur, of subtle and infinite caprice.

After a time she grew to love us, as a cat loves, with no docility, but with an unalterable and touching constancy, which well deserves that I should hold her memory dear. In the spring, when the pale March sun warmed the chilly earth, she had the ever-repeated delight of watching Suleïma, the tortoise, her friend and fellow guest, crawl down the garden paths. In the lovely May weather she

grew bold and restless, wearying of her austere surroundings, and escaping more than once to wander
over the neighbouring roofs. In the summer time
she was languid as a Creole, drowsing for hours on
the wall beneath the honeysuckle and roses, or sun-
ning herself on the white stones between the pots
of flowering cactus. Exquisitely and fastidiously
neat, sedate in manner, an aristocrat to the tips of
her little claws, she so hated other cats that the
advent of a visitor put all her serenity to flight.
In her own domain she suffered no intrusion. If
over the garden wall two little ears were raised,
two little eyes peeped furtively, if a rustling in the
branches, a trembling of the ivy leaves awakened
her suspicion, her fur bristled, and she sprang like
a young Fury at the stranger. Nothing could re-
strain her, and presently we, the listeners, would
hear the sound of scuffling, a fall, and lamentable
cries. On the whole, an independent and somewhat
lawless cat; but affectionate and caressing, eager to
roam, and still more glad to return to us when her
vagabond excursions were over.

Moumoutte Blanche was five years old, in the
flower of her beauty, and I had grown attached to
her as a member of the family and a household
god, when, from the Gulf of Pekin, three thousand
leagues away, there came one who was destined to

be her inseparable friend, the strange, bizarre, humbly born little cat, Moumoutte Chinoise.

Vies de Deux Chattes, PIERRE LOTI.

Moumoutte Chinoise

I REMEMBER the day when the Chinese cat and I established friendly relations. It was a melancholy afternoon in September. The first fogs of autumn were brooding over the cold, unquiet waters. We were sailing eastward, and the ship creaked plaintively as she slid into the hollows of the sea. I sat writing in the obscurity of my cabin, which grew darker and darker as the green waves washed over my closed port-hole.

Suddenly a little form came stealing out of the shadows. It drew nearer, stealthily and hesitatingly. There was an oriental grace in its fashion of holding one paw suspended in air, as though uncertain where to place it next. It looked at me with anxious interrogation.

"What does the cat want?" I said to myself. She has had her dinner. She is not hungry. What is it she is after?"

As though to answer me, *la Chinoise* crept closer and closer, until she was at my feet. Then sitting upright, and curling her tail about her, she uttered a gentle little cry, looking straight into my eyes which seemed to hold some message she could read. She understood that I was a thinking creature, capable of pity, accessible to a mute prayer, and that my eyes were mirrors in which her troubled soul must study my good or bad designs. It is terrifying to think how near an animal is to us when it can realize such things.

For the first time I looked attentively at the little visitor who for two weeks had shared my lodgings. She was tawny as a wild hare, and striped like a tiger. Her face and neck were white. Certainly an ugly and a miserable cat; but her very ugliness had in it something strange and appealing, something which contrasted pleasantly with the comely cats of France. Her movements were stealthy and sinuous, her great ears stood erect, her tail was long and ragged, her eyes alone were beautiful, the deep golden eyes of the East, restless and full of expression.

While I watched her, I carelessly laid my hand on her head, and stroked the yellow fur. It was not mere physical pleasure she felt in the caress, but a sense of protection, of sympathy in her abandonment. It was for this she had crept from her hiding-place; it was for this, and not for food and drink, that she had come, wistful and terrified, to beg. Her little cat soul implored some company, some friendship in a lonely world.

Where had she learned this need, poor outcast, never before touched by a kindly hand, never the object of affection, unless, indeed, the paternal junk held some forlorn Chinese child, as joyless, as famished, as friendless as herself; a child who, perishing perchance in that miserable abode, would leave no more trace of its incomplete existence than she had done.

At last one small paw was lifted, oh, so delicately, so discreetly, and after a long, anxious look, Moumoutte, believing the time had now come for venturing all things, took heart of grace, and leaped upon my knee.

There she curled herself, but with tact and reserve, seeming to make her little body as light as possible, a mere featherweight, and never taking her eyes from my face. She stayed a long time, inconveniencing me greatly; but I lacked the courage to put her down, as I should have done had she been pretty and gay. Nervously aware of my least movement, she watched me intently, not as though fearing I would do her harm,— she was too intelligent to think me capable of such a thing,— but as though to ask, "Are you sure I do not weary or offend you?" Then her disquietude softened into cajolery, and her eyes, lifted to mine, said with charming distinctness: "On this autumn evening, so dreary to the soul of a cat, since we two are isolated in this unquiet abode, and lost amid infinite dangers, let us bestow upon each other a little of that mysterious something which sweetens misery and quiets death, which is called affection, and which expresses itself from time to time in a caress."

Vies de Deux Chattes, PIERRE LOTI.

The Two Cats

THE spring was clear and beautiful, the air loud with the song of birds, and to Moumoutte Chinoise, reared in suffocating darkness, the bright sunshine, the soft winds, and the presence of other cats were both a mystery and a delight. She explored the garden from end to end, smelling the young blades of grass, and the tiny leaves that came shooting up from the warm earth. All that was so fámiliar to us was to her new and strange; and Moumoutte Blanche, once the sole ruler of this lovely place, shared with her its endless wonders.

The borders of the miniature lake pleased *la Chinoise* best of all. She picked her careful way through the grass, which grew taller day by day; she crawled on her belly, as though tracking down her quarry; she hid behind the lilliputian rocks, and crouched under the ivy, for all the world like a little tiger in a jungle. I amused myself by watching her slow progress, her frequent pauses, her bewilderment; and, whenever she caught me looking at her, she turned and faced me, immovable as a statue, with one paw delicately held in air. Her droll yellow eyes fixed upon my face said as plainly as words could do: " You will permit me to continue my stroll? See how lightly and carefully I walk. And don't you think that everything here is very pretty? These paths, and these strange little green things which smell so good? And then those other objects I see above me, which are called the sun, the moon, the stars. How different it is from our old lodgings, and how well off we are, you and I, in this country."

.   .   .   .

In the winter our cats became our fireside guests, our constant companions, sharing with us, not only the warmth and flicker of the flames, but the vague melancholy of our twilight reveries, and our unfathomable dreams. This, too, is the time of their greatest beauty. At the first approach of cold weather, Moumoutte Chinoise patched up the holes in her ragged coat, and Moumoutte Blanche adorned herself with an imposing cravat, a snow white boa, which framed her little face like some vast Medicean ruff. The friendship of the two cats for each other grew stronger in such close companionship. In the depth of an armchair, or on their cushions before the fire, they slept for days together, rolled up into one big furry ball, without visible head or tail.

It was Moumoutte Chinoise who perseveringly courted this comfortable warmth. When, after a short and chilly run in the garden, she found her

friend sleeping by the fire, she would steal up to
her very softly, and with as much caution as if she
were stalking a mouse. Moumoutte Blanche, always nervous, pettish, and averse to being disturbed, would sometimes resent the intrusion, and
give her a gentle slap by way of remonstrance. It
was never returned. *La Chinoise* would merely
lift her little paw with a mocking gesture, looking
at me meanwhile out of the tails of her eyes, as
though to say: " She has a difficult temper, hasn't
she; but you know I never take her seriously."
Then with gentle determination she would nestle
resolutely by Blanche's side, and bury her head in
the soft white fur. Her glance of drowsy triumph
expressed the fulness of her content. " This is
what I was after," it said, " and here I am."

Vies de Deux Chattes, PIERRE LOTI.

Eponine

EPONINE is a small cat, very delicately made. Her eyes have the oblique slant of the Chinese, and are sea-green like the eyes of Pallas Athene; her little velvety nose looks like a fine truffle of Périgord; her physiognomy is charmingly expressive; her superb fur is of a deep and lustrous black. Never was cat more nervous, sensitive and sympathetic. Never was cat more charged with electricity. If you stroke her smooth back on a winter night, tiny blue sparks flash beneath your hand. She is the soul of hospitality, and delights to receive my visitors, leading the way into the salon, and entertaining them as best she can with polite little sounds, intended for conversation. "Do not be impatient," she tries to say, "Monsieur is coming down. Look at the pictures, or, if I amuse you, talk to me." When I enter, she retires discreetly to an armchair, or a corner of the piano, and listens to the conversation without interrupting it, as one accustomed from kittenhood to good society.

At breakfast and at dinner Eponine sits by my side, being permitted, because she is so small, to rest her fore-paws on the extreme edge of the table. She has her own plate and tumbler, and she waits her turn to be helped, behaving with a gentleness and decency which might be imitated by many children.   She is very punctual, coming as soon as she hears the bell; and, when I enter the dining-room, I find her already in her place, her paws folded on the tablecloth, her smooth forehead held up to be kissed, like a well-bred little girl who is politely affectionate to relatives and old people.

Eponine is passionately fond of fish, and sometimes, when by careful investigation in the kitchen she has ascertained that there is fish to come, she refuses, after the fashion of children eager for dessert, to touch her plate of soup.   On such occasions I say to her coldly: " Mademoiselle, a young lady who is not hungry for soup is not expected to have any appetite for fish," and the dish is carried pitilessly past her eager little nose. Once convinced that I am in earnest, Eponine, like the glutton that she is, laps up her soup hastily, swallows every crumb of bread, and then looks at me with the complacent air of one who has acquitted herself of her duty, and whose conscience is free from reproach.   Her portion of fish is then served to her, and she eats it with well-merited enjoyment, finishing her repast with a little drink of water.

When I am giving a dinner, Eponine does not

96

need to wait until the guests arrive, to make sure
of this fact. As soon as she sees that knife, fork
and spoon are lying by her plate, she assumes that
she is not expected at table, and retires without
umbrage to the piano stool, which is her refuge on
such occasions. Those who deny that animals are
capable of reasoning may explain this conduct as
best they can. My observant and judicious little
cat perceives at her place certain utensils which are
used only by human beings, and therefore con-
cludes that she must this day resign her privileges
in favour of a visitor. She never suffers herself to
be mistaken; but now and then, if she recognizes an
old friend, she will leap upon his knee, and intimate
that she is ready to accept any choice morsel which
he may be disposed to share with her.

Ménagerie Intime, THÉOPHILE GAUTIER.

Don Pierrot de Navarre

PIERROT received his name in kittenhood, on account of his immaculate whiteness. His title was added later, and was a tribute to his size and majesty of demeanour. He had a charming disposition, and shared our family life with an intimacy which is possible only to cats who are treated with gentleness and consideration. Sitting close to the fire, he seemed always interested in the conversation, and now and then, as he looked from one speaker to another, he would give a little protesting mew, as though in remonstrance to some opinion which he could not bring himself to share. He adored books, and whenever he found one open on the table, he would sit down by it, look attentively at the printed page, turn over a leaf or two, and finally fall asleep, for all the world as if he had been trying to read a modern novel. As soon as he saw me sit down to write, he would jump on my desk, and watch the crooked and fantastic figures which my pen scattered over the paper, turning his head every time I began a fresh line. Sometimes it occurred to him to take a part in my work, and then he would make little clutches at my pen, with the evident design of writing a page or so; for he was an æsthetic cat like Hoffman's Murr, and I

98

more than half suspect him of composing a volume of memoirs, scribbling feverishly at night in some remote gutter by the light of his own gleaming eyes. Alas, that such compositions should have been lost forever!

Don Pierrot never went to bed until I came home at night. I found him always waiting for me at the door, and he received me with enthusiasm, rubbing himself against my legs, arching his back, and purring a loud welcome. Then he would stalk before me like a groom of the chamber, prepared no doubt to carry my candle had I entrusted it to him. He slept on the headboard of my bed, perched safely like a bird on a bough; but in the early morning would descend from this lofty station, and lie patiently by my side until it was time to get up.

On one point Pierrot was inflexible. Like the concierge, he considered that midnight was quite late enough for me to be abroad. It so happened, however, that the little club known as the " Society of the Four Candles," because four candles in four silver candlesticks lit up the four corners of the table, was formed about this time; and our discussions were often so prolonged and so engrossing that, like Cinderella, we took no count of the hour. For several nights Pierrot waited up for me until two o'clock; then, seriously concerned, he marked his displeasure by going to bed and to sleep without me. I was so touched by this mute protest against my innocent dissipations that I resolved to amend my ways; but it was a long time before I could convince Pierrot that my conversion was sincere. Many nights of unbroken punctuality were needed to restore his confidence, and induce him to take up his old post by the door, and to receive me with his old urbanity.

It is no easy task to win the friendship of a cat. He is a philosopher, sedate, tranquil, a creature of habit, a lover of decency and order. He does not bestow his regard lightly, and, though he may consent to be your companion, he will never be your slave. Even in his most affectionate moods he preserves his freedom, and refuses a servile obedience. But once gain his absolute confidence, and he is a friend for life. He shares your hours of work, of solitude, of melancholy. He spends whole evenings on your knee, purring and dozing, content with your silence, and spurning for your sake the society of his kind. In vain loud miaulings from the neighbouring roof summon him to those choice entertainments where red herrings take the place of tea. He pays no heed, and cannot be tempted from your side. If you put him down, he leaps back again, mewing a gentle protest.

From time to time he looks into your face with eyes so human, so full of understanding and regard, that you are smitten by fear. Can it be possible that there is no thought behind that absorbed and mysterious scrutiny?

Ménagerie Intime, THÉOPHILE GAUTIER.

Nero

I owN that when Agrippina brought her first-
born son — aged two days — and established him
in my bedroom closet, the plan struck me at the
start as inconvenient. I had prepared another
nursery for the little Claudius Nero, and I en-
deavoured for a while to convince his mother that
my arrangements were best. But Agrippina was
inflexible. The closet suited her in every respect;
and, with charming and irresistible flattery, she
gave me to understand in the mute language I
knew so well that she wished her baby boy to be
under my immediate protection. "I bring him to
you because I trust you," she said as plainly as
looks can speak. "Downstairs they handle him all
the time, and it is not good for kittens to be han-
dled. Here he is safe from harm, and here he
shall remain." After a few weak remonstrances,
the futility of which I too clearly understood, her
persistence carried the day. I removed my cloth-
ing from the closet, laid a rug upon the floor,
had the door taken from its hinges, and resigned
myself for the first time in my life to the daily and
hourly companionship of an infant.

I was amply rewarded. People who require their
household cat to rear her offspring in some remote

attic, or dark corner of the cellar, have no idea of all the diversion and pleasure that they lose. It is delightful to watch the little blind, sprawling, feeble, helpless things develop swiftly into the grace and agility of kittenhood. It is delightful to see the mingled pride and anxiety of the mother, whose parental love increases with every hour of care, and who exhibits her young family as if they were infant Gracchi, the hope of all their race. During Nero's extreme youth, there were times, I admit, when Agrippina wearied both of his companionship and of her own maternal duties. Once or twice she abandoned him at night for the greater luxury of my bed, where she slept tranquilly by my side, unmindful of the little wailing cries with which Nero lamented her desertion. Once or twice the heat of early summer tempted her to spend the evening on the piazza roof which lay beneath my windows, and I have passed some anxious hours awaiting her return, and wondering what would happen if she never came back, and I were left to bring up the baby by hand.

But as the days sped on, and Nero grew rapidly in beauty and intelligence, Agrippina's affection for him knew no bounds. She could hardly bear to leave him, even for a little while, and always came hurrying back to him with a loud, frightened mew, as if fearing he might have been stolen in her absence. At night she purred over him for hours, or made little gurgling noises expressive of ineffable content. She resented the careless curiosity of strangers, and was a trifle supercilious when the cook stole softly in to give vent to her fervent admiration. But from first to last she shared with me her pride and pleasure; and the joy in her beautiful eyes, as she raised them to mine, was frankly confiding and sympathetic. When the infant Claudius rolled for the first time over the ledge of the closet, and lay sprawling on the bedroom floor, it would have been hard to say which of us was the more elated at his prowess. A narrow pink ribbon of honour was at once tied around the small adventurer's neck, and he was pronounced the most daring and agile of kittens. From that day his brief career was a series of brilliant triumphs.

A Kitten, AGNES REPPLIER.

Calvin

I HESITATE a little to speak of Calvin's capacity for friendship, and of the affectionateness of his nature, for I know, from his own reserve, that he would not care to have it much talked about. We understood each other perfectly, but we never made any fuss about it. When I spoke his name and snapped my fingers, he came to me; when I returned home at night he was pretty sure to be waiting for me near the gate, and would rise and saunter along the walk, as if his being there were purely accidental,— so shy was he commonly of showing feeling; and when I opened the door, he never rushed in like a cat, but loitered and lounged, as if he had had no intention of going in, but would condescend to. And yet the fact was he knew dinner was ready, and he was bound to be there. He kept the run of dinner-time. It happened sometimes, during our absence in the summer, that dinner would be early, and Calvin, walking about the grounds, missed it, and came in late. But he did not make a mistake the second day. There was one thing he never did,— he never rushed through an open doorway. He never forgot his dignity. If he had asked to have the door opened, and was eager to go out, he always went deliberately. I can see him now, standing on the sill, looking about at the sky, as if he were thinking whether it were worth while to take an umbrella, until he was near having his tail shut in.

His friendship was constant rather than demonstrative. When we returned from an absence of nearly two years, Calvin welcomed us with evident pleasure, but showed his satisfaction rather by tranquil happiness than by fuming about. He had the faculty of making us glad to get home. It was his constancy that was so attractive. He liked companionship, but he wouldn't be petted, or fussed over, or sit in any one's lap a moment; he always extricated himself from such familiarity with dignity, and with no show of temper. If there was any petting to be done, however, he chose to do it. Often he would sit looking at me, and then, moved by a delicate affection, come and pull at my coat and sleeve until he could touch my face with his nose, and then go away contented. He had a habit of coming to my study in the morning, sitting quietly by my side or on the table for hours, watching the pen run over the paper, occasionally swinging his tail round for a blotter, and then going to sleep among the papers by the inkstand. Or, more rarely, he would watch the writing from a perch on my shoulder. Writing

106

always interested him, and, until he understood it, he wanted to hold the pen.

He always held himself in a kind of reserve with his friend, as if he had said, "Let us respect our personality, and not make a ' mess ' of friendship." He saw, with Emerson, the risk of degrading it to trivial conveniency. "Why insist on rash personal relations with your friend? Leave this touching and clawing." Yet I would not give an unfair notion of his aloofness, his fine sense of the sacredness of the me and the not-me. And, at the risk of not being believed, I will relate an incident which was often repeated. Calvin had the practice of passing a portion of the night in the contemplation of its beauties, and would come into our chamber over the roof of the conservatory through the open window, summer and winter, and go to sleep on the foot of my bed. He would do this always exactly in the same way; he never was content to stay in the chamber if we compelled him to go upstairs and through the door. He had the obstinacy of General Grant. In the morning, he performed his toilet, and went down to breakfast with the rest of the family. Now, when the mistress was absent from home, and at no other time, Calvin would come in the morning, when the bell rang, to the head of the bed, put up his forepaws and look into my face, follow me about when I rose, " assist " at the dressing, and in many purring ways show his fondness, as if he had plainly said, " I know that she has gone away, but I am here." Such was Calvin in rare moments.

CHARLES DUDLEY WARNER.

THE CAT

Corporation Cats

CATS are the only animals which are ever really
owned by clubs and corporations. A dog, if it
nominally belongs to a company of men, is really
the property of some individual man. It must
have a master. A cat, being always its own master, lives happily under a corporate body. Some
of the lordliest and most self-satisfied beasts I have
ever known were club and college cats. A cat be-
longing to one of the London dock companies was
almost ridiculous (if a cat could be ridiculous)
from the airs of possession and self-importance
which it assumed in regard to the company's vaults.
Sir Frederick Pollock has shown us, in the " Senior
Fellow," to what a pitch of dignity a college cat
may rise when it is once on the foundation of a
learned society.

The Spectator.

Tom of Corpus

The Junior Fellow's vows were said;
Among his co-mates and their Head
    His place was fairly set,
Of welcome from friends old and new
Full dues he had, and more than due;
    What could be lacking yet?

One said, " The Senior Fellow's vote! "
The Senior Fellow, black of coat,
    Save where his front was white,
Arose and sniffed the stranger's shoes
With critic nose, as ancients use
    To judge mankind aright.

I — for 'twas I who tell the tale —
Conscious of fortune's trembling scale,
    Awaited the decree;
But Tom had judged: " He loves our race; "
And, as to his ancestral place,
    He leapt upon my knee.

Thenceforth in common-room and hall,
A *verus socius* known to all,
    I came and went and sat,
Far from cross fate or envy's reach,
For none a title could impeach,
    Accepted by the cat.

While statutes changed, and freshmen came,
His gait, his wisdom were the same,
    His age no more than mellow;
Yet nothing mortal may defy
The march of *Anno Domini,*
    Not e'en the Senior Fellow.

Beneath our linden shade he lies;
Mere eld hath softly closed his eyes
    With late and honoured end.
He seems, while catless we confer,
To join with faint Elysian purr,
    A tutelary friend.

SIR FREDERICK POLLOCK.

Oliver

A LONG series of cats has reigned over my household for the last forty years or thereabouts. The present occupant of the throne is a large, young, grey Tabby,— Oliver by name. Not that he is in any sense a Protector, for I doubt whether he has the heart to kill a mouse. However, I saw him catch and eat the first butterfly of the season, and trust that the germ of courage, thus manifested, may develop with age into efficient mousing.

As to sagacity, I should say that his judgment respecting the warmest place and the softest cushion in a room is infallible, his punctuality at meal times is admirable, and his pertinacity in jumping on people's shoulders till they give him some of the best of what is going, indicates great firmness.

THOMAS HUXLEY *to Mr. J. G. Kitton.*

Oliver

I WISH you would write seriously to M——. She is not behaving well to Oliver. I have seen handsomer kittens, but few more lively and energetically destructive. Just now he scratched away at something that M—— says cost 13s. 6d. a yard, and reduced more or less of it to combings.

M—— therefore excludes him from the dining-room, and from all those opportunities of higher education which he would naturally have in *my* house.

I have argued that it is as immoral to place 13s. 6d. a yardnesses within reach of kittens as to hang bracelets and diamond rings in the front garden. But in vain. Oliver is banished, and the protector (not Oliver) is sat upon. In truth and justice aid your Pa.

THOMAS HUXLEY *to his youngest daughter.*

Mentu

THE wild nature in Mentu is as strong as his inbred civilization; and the two are at strife together. His heart and his appetite lead him back and back to the house; keep him there for days together, a dainty fine gentleman, warm-hearted, capricious. But the spirit of the wild creature rises in him, and the night comes when, at bedtime, no Mentu is waiting at the door to be let in; or in the evening, as he hears the wind rise and stir the branches, even while the rain beats on the window pane, the compelling power of out-of-doors is on him, and he must go; and when the window is lifted, and the night air streams in, there is but one leap into the darkness.

He will return early in the morning, tired and satiate, or spring in some evening as the dusk gathers, with gleaming eyes where the light of the wild woods flickers and dies down in the comfortable firelight of an English home.

This is the true cat, the real Mentu, this wild creature who must go on his mysterious errands; or who, I rather believe it, plunges out to revel in the intoxication of innumerable scents, unaccounted sounds, and the half-revealed forms of wood and field in twilight, in darkness, or in dawn. In his soul he is a dramatist, an artist in sensation. He lives with human beings, he loves them, as we live with children and love them, and play their games. But the great world calls us, and we must go; and Mentu's business in life is elsewhere. He lives in the half-lights, in secret places, free and alone,— this mysterious little-great being whom his mistress calls " My cat."

The Soul of a Cat
MARGARET BENSON.

The Shah of Persia

CATS of his perfect beauty, of his perfect grace, possibly might be found, Madame Jolicœur grudgingly admitted, in the Persian royal catteries; but nowhere else in the Orient, and nowhere at all in the Occident, she declared with an energetic conviction, possibly could there be a cat who even approached him in intellectual development, in wealth of interesting accomplishments, and, above all, in natural sweetness of disposition,— a sweetness so marked that even under extreme provocation he never had been known to thrust out an angry paw. This is not to say that the *Shah de Perse* was a characterless cat, a lymphatic nonentity. On occasions — usually in connection with food that was distasteful to him — he could have his resentments; but they were manifested always with a dignified restraint. His nearest approach to ill-mannered abruptness was to bat with a contemptuous paw the offending morsel from his plate; which brusque act he followed by fixing upon the bestower of unworthy food a coldly, but always politely contemptuous stare. Ordinarily, however, his displeasure was exhibited by no more overt action than his retirement to a corner,— he had his choice in corners, governed by the intensity of his feelings,— and there seating himself with his back turned scornfully to an offending world. Even in his kindliest corner, on such occasions, the expression of his scornful back was as a whole volume of winged words.

But the rare little cat tantrums of the *Shah de Perse* — if to his so gentle excesses may be applied so strong a term — were but as sun-spots on the effulgence of his otherwise constant amiability. The regnant desires by which his worthy little life was governed were to love and to please. He was the most cuddlesome cat, Madame Jolicœur unhesitatingly asserted, that ever had lived; and he had a purr — softly thunderous and winningly affectionate — that was in keeping with his cuddlesome ways. When, of his own volition, he would jump into her abundant lap, and go burrowing with his soft little round head beneath her soft round elbows, the while gurglingly purring forth his love for her, Madame Jolicœur, quite justifiably, at times was moved to tears. Equally was his sweet nature exhibited in his always eager willingness to show off his little train of cat accomplishments. He would give his paw with a courteous grace to any lady or gentleman — he drew the caste line rigidly — who asked for it. For his mistress, he would spring to a considerable height, and clutch

117

with his two soft paws — never by any mistake scratching — her outstretched wrist; and so would remain suspended while he delicately nibbled from between her fingers her edible offering. For her, he would make an almost painfully real pretence of being a dead cat; extending himself upon the rug with an exaggeratedly death-like rigidity,— and so remaining until her command to be alive again brought him briskly to rub himself, rising on his hind legs and purring mellowly, against her comfortable knee.

Madame Jolicœur's Cat.

THOMAS A. JANVIER.

Peter; an Elegy

In vain the kindly call, in vain
The plate for which thou once wast fain,
At morn, and noon, and daylight's wane,
    O King of mousers!
No more I hear thee purr and purr,
As in the frolic days that were,
When thou didst rub thy velvet fur
    Against my trousers.

How empty are the places where
Thou erst wert frankly debonair,
Nor dreamed a dream of feline care,
    A capering kitten.
The sunny haunts where, grown a cat,
You pondered this, considered that,
The cushioned chair, the rug, the mat,
    By firelight smitten.

Although of few you stood in dread,
How well you knew a friendly tread,
And what upon your back and head
    The stroking hand meant.

A passing scent could keenly wake
Thy eagerness for chop or steak,
Yet, Puss, how rarely didst thou break
    The eighth commandment.

Though brief thy life, a little span
Of days compared with that of man,
The time allotted to thee ran
    In smoother metre.
Now, with the warm earth o'er thy breast,
O wisest of thy kind, and best,
Forever mayst thou softly rest,
    In pace, Peter.

CLINTON SCOLLARD.

Peace and War

THE strong enmity which exists between my otherwise gentle and amiable cats is not unknown to you. When you left us, the result of many a fierce conflict was that Hurley remained master of the green and garden, Rumpel always retiring, upon the appearance of his victorious enemy, into the house, as to a citadel or sanctuary. The conqueror was perhaps indebted for this superiority to his hardier habits, living always in the open air, and providing for himself; while Rumpel (who, though born under a bailiff's roof, was, nevertheless, kittened with a silver spoon in his mouth) passes his hours in luxurious repose beside the fire, and looks for his meals as punctually as any two-legged member of the family.

· · · · · · · · ·

Some weeks ago Hurlyburlybuss was manifestly emaciated and enfeebled by ill-health, and Rumpelstilzchen with great magnanimity made overtures of peace. The whole progress of the treaty was seen from the parlour window;—the caution with which Rumpel made his advances, the sullen dignity with which they were received, their mutual uneasiness when Rumpel, after a slow and wary approach, seated himself whisker-to-whisker by his rival, the mutual fear which restrained, not only teeth and claws, but even all tones of defiance, the mutual agitation of their tails, and lastly the manner in which Hurley retreated, like Ajax, still keeping his face towards his old antagonist. The overture, I fear, was not received as generously as it was made; for no sooner had Hurlyburlybuss recovered strength than hostilities were recommenced with greater violence than ever; Rumpel, who had not abused his superiority when he possessed it, having acquired meantime a confidence which made him keep the field.

Dreadful were the combats which ensued, as their ears, faces and legs bear witness. We are often obliged to interfere and separate them. Oh, it is awful to hear the note with which they prelude their encounters. The long, low growl slowly rises and swells until it becomes a yowl, and then it is snapped short by a sound which seems as though they were spitting fire and venom at each other. All means of reconciling them, and making them understand how goodly a thing it is for cats to dwell together in peace, are in vain. The proceedings of the Society for the Abolishment of War are not more utterly ineffectual and hopeless.

Memoir of the Cats of Greta Hall.
ROBERT SOUTHEY.

The Freebooter

Cats I scorn, who, sleek and fat,
Shiver at a Norway rat.
Rough and hardy, bold and free,
Be the cat that's made for me;
He whose nervous paw can take
My lady's lapdog by the neck;
With furious hiss attack the hen,
And snatch a chicken from the pen.

DR. ERASMUS DARWIN.

Cat Tales

I observe
authors who speak
concerning cats with a
familiarity and a levity
most distasteful.

Andrew Lang

Sad Memories

They tell me I am beautiful, they praise my silken
  hair,
My little feet that silently slip on from stair to stair;
They praise my pretty, trustful face, and innocent
  grey eye;
Fond hands caress me oftentimes,— yet would that I
  might die!

Why was I born to be abhorr'd of man, and bird, and
  beast?
The bulfinch marks me stealing by, and straight his
  song hath ceased;
The shrewmouse eyes me shudderingly, then flees;
  and, worse than that,
The house-dog he flees after me,— why was I born a
  cat?

Men prize the heartless hound who quits dry-eyed his
  native land,
Who wags a mercenary tail, and licks a tyrant hand.
The leal true cat they prize not, that, if e'er compell'd
  to roam,
Still flies, when let out of the bag, precipitately home.

They call me cruel. Do I know if mouse or song-
  bird feels?

I only know they make me light and salutary meals;
And if — as 'tis my nature to — ere I devour, I tease
'em,
Why should a low-bred gardener's boy pursue me with
a besom?

Should china fall, or chandeliers, or anything but
stocks,—
Nay, stocks when they're in flower-pots, the cat ex-
pects hard knocks;
Should ever anything be missed,— milk, coals, um-
brellas, brandy,
The cat's pitched into with a boot, or anything that's
handy.

" I remember, I remember," how one night I " fleeted
by,"
And gain'd the blessed tiles, and gazed into the cold,
clear sky.
" I remember, I remember, how my little lovers
came,"
And there, beneath the crescent moon, play'd many a
little game.

They fought! by good St. Catherine, 'twas a fearful
sight to see
The coal-black crest, the glowering orbs, of one gi-
gantic He.

128

Like bow by some tall bowman bent at Hastings or
    Poictiers,
His huge back curved till none observed a vestige of
    his ears.

He stood, an ebon crescent, flouting that ivory moon,
Then raised the pibroch of his race, the Song without
    a Tune;
Gleam'd his white teeth, his mammoth tail waved
    darkly to and fro,
As with one complex yell he burst, all claws, upon
    the foe.

It thrills me now, that final Miaow, that weird, un-
    earthly din;
Lone maidens heard it far away, and leap'd out of
    their skin;
A pot-boy from his den o'erhead peep'd with a scared,
    wan face,
Then sent a random brickbat down, which knock'd
    me into space.

Nine days I fell,— or thereabouts,— and, had we not
    nine lives,
I wis I ne'er had seen again thy sausage-shop, St.
    Ives!
Had I, as some cats have, nine tails, how gladly I
    would lick

The hand, and person generally, of him who heaved
    that brick!

For me they fill the milk-bowl up, and cull the choice
    sardine;
But ah! I nevermore shall be the cat I once have been!
The memories of that fatal night they haunt me even
    now;
In dreams I see that rampant He, and tremble at that
    Miaow.

CHARLES STUART CALVERLEY.

The Young Man and His Cat

A YOUNG man owned a cat with which he was wont to sport, and which he greatly loved. Day and night he prayed to Venus, that she would show favour to him and to his cherished pet. The kindly goddess heard his prayer, and changed the cat into the most beautiful of maidens, whom the youth married that very day. But alas! even on their wedding night, when the bride lay clasped in her husband's arms, she heard a mouse scamper across the room, and leaped lightly from her bed to pursue it. Venus, angry at this profanation of wifehood, and perceiving that, however altered in form, a cat remains a cat at heart, changed her back into a beast, in order that soul and body might be in conformity.

Æsop's Fables.

The Ratcatcher and Cats

The rats by night such mischief did,
Betty was every morning chid.
They undermined whole sides of bacon,
Her cheese was sapped, her tarts were taken;
Her pasties, fenced with thickest paste,
Were all demolished and laid waste.
She cursed the Cat for want of duty,
Who left her foes a constant booty.

    An engineer of noted skill
Engaged to stop the growing ill;
From room to room he now surveys
Their haunts, their works, their secret ways;
Finds where they scape an ambuscade,
And whence the nightly sally's made.
An envious Cat from place to place,
Unseen, attends his silent pace.
She saw that, if his trade went on,
The purring race must be undone;
So secretly removes his baits,
And every stratagem defeats.

    Again he sets the poisoned toils,
    And Puss again the labour foils.
"What foe (to frustrate my designs)
My schemes thus nightly countermines?"
Incensed he cries; "this very hour
The wretch shall bleed beneath my power."

So said,— a ponderous trap he brought,
And in the fact poor Puss was caught.
"Smuggler," says he, "thou shalt be made
A victim to our loss of trade."

The captive Cat, with piteous mews,
For pardon, life, and freedom sues.
"A sister of the science spare!
One interest is our common care."
"What insolence!" the Man replied;
"Shall Cats with us the game divide?
Were all your interloping band
Extinguished, or expelled the land,
We Rat-catchers might raise our fees,
Sole guardians of a nation's cheese!"

A Cat who saw the lifted knife,
Thus spoke, and saved her sister's life:
"In every age and clime, we see
Two of a trade can ne'er agree;
Each hates his neighbour for encroaching,
Squire stigmatizes squire for poaching;
Beauties with beauties are in arms,
And scandal pelts each other's charms;
Kings, too, their neighbour kings dethrone,
In hope to make the world their own.

But let us limit our desires,
Nor war like beauties, kings, and squires;
For, though we both one prey pursue,
There's game enough for us and you."

JOHN GAY.

A Captain's Kitten

A MOST tragical incident fell out this day at
sea. While the ship was under sail, but making,
as will appear, no great way, a kitten, one of the
four feline inhabitants of the cabin, fell from the
window into the water. An alarm was immediately
given to the captain, who was then upon deck,
and who received it with many bitter oaths. He
immediately gave orders to the steersman in favour
of the poor thing, as he called it; the sails were
instantly slackened, and all hands employed to re-
cover the animal. I was, I own, surprised at this;
less, indeed, at the captain's extreme tenderness,
than at his conceiving any possibility of success;
for if Puss had had nine thousand instead of nine
lives, I concluded they had all been lost. The
boatswain, however, was more sanguine; for having stripped himself of his jacket, breeches, and
shirt, he leaped boldly into the water, and, to my
great astonishment, in a few minutes returned to
the ship, bearing the motionless animal in his
mouth. Nor was this, I observed, a matter of such
great difficulty as it appeared to my ignorance, and
possibly may seem to that of my fresh-water
reader. The kitten was now exposed to air and sun
on the deck, where its life, of which it retained no
symptoms, was despaired of by all.

The captain's humanity did not so totally destroy his philosophy as to make him yield himself up to affliction. Having felt his loss like a man, he resolved to show he could bear it like one; and, after declaring he had rather have lost a cask of rum or brandy, he betook himself to threshing at backgammon with the Portuguese friar, in which innocent amusement they passed their leisure hours.

Journal of a Voyage to Lisbon
HENRY FIELDING.

THE CAT

A Sailor

A SHIP cat loves its home as unswervingly as does the happier animal whose lot is cast amid gardens and moonlit walls. To the landsman's prejudiced eye there is little choice in boats, especially in the dismal and dirty cargo boats " that sail the wet seas roun'." They may be " England's pride," but, as permanent habitations, they seem to lack everything that would appeal to the refined instincts and restless habits of a cat. Yet Pussy is as faithful to her " hollow oak " as poets have ever pretended to be, and will not barter its manifold discomforts for the pleasant firesides of earth. A very beautiful cat, carried in infancy from some remote village in the Apennines, was given as a mascot to the Italian captain of an oil-tank steamer which ran between Savona and Point Breeze, Philadelphia. In the course of time she presented the ship with a family of kittens, who were less than a month old when the Philadelphia docks were reached. Like other sailors, Pussy indulged in some irregularities while on shore; and, as the result of prolonged dissipation, she was found to be missing when the *Bayonne* was loaded, and ready to depart. Search was made in vain about the wharves; and Captain Hugo was compelled, not only to sail

137

without his mascot, but to assume the responsibility for her abandoned infants.

Two days later the prodigal came back. Another and a larger boat filled the *Bayonne's* place. Repentant and dismayed, she visited every steamer in the docks; then, convinced that her indiscretions had made her both homeless and kittenless, she took up her quarters in a watch-box, and patiently awaited Captain Hugo's return. Week followed week; scores of barks arrived, and were each in turn anxiously inspected; and still, undiscouraged by repeated disappointments, she bravely kept her post. At last the *Bayonne* was sighted, and there was no need this time to hunt for the cat. There she stood, quivering with agitation, on the extreme edge of the wharf, as the malodorous little craft plied its way along the river. The captain's big black dog, Pussy's old friend and companion, barked his furious welcome from the deck. The sound increased her excitement, and, when the steamer was still twelve feet from the docks, she cleared with flying leap the intervening space, and, mid the cheers of the crew, ran straight to the captain's cabin where she had left her kittens three months before. They were well-grown young cats by this time, and disposed to resent her intrusion;

but the mother's joy was as excessive as if she had been parted from them for but a single night.

The Fireside Sphinx

AGNES REPPLIER.

The Point of View

" Dog," said the Cat to a little fat spaniel coiled up on a rug, like a lady's muff with a head and tail stuck on to it ; " Dog, what do you make of it all? "

The Dog opened his languid eyes, looked sleepily at the Cat for a moment, and dropped them again.

" Dog," said the Cat, " I want to talk to you ; don't go to sleep. Can't you answer a civil question? "

" Don't bother me," said the Dog. " I am tired. I stood on my hind legs ten minutes this morning before I could get my breakfast, and it hasn't agreed with me."

" Who told you to do it? " said the Cat.

" Why, the lady I have to take care of me," replied the Dog.

" Do you feel any better for it, Dog, after you have been standing on your hind legs? "

" Haven't I told you, you stupid Cat, that it hasn't agreed with me? Let me go to sleep, and don't plague me."

" But I mean," persisted the Cat, " do you feel improved, as human beings call it? They tell their children that if they will do what they are told, they will improve, and grow good and great. Do you feel good and great? "

"How do I know?" said the Dog. "I eat my breakfast, and am content. Let me alone!"

"Do you never think, O Dog without a soul! Do you never wonder what dogs are, and what this world is?"

The Dog stretched himself, and rolled his eyes lazily around the room. "I conceive," he said, "that the world is for dogs, and that men and women are put into it to take care of dogs; women to take care of little dogs like me, and men for the big dogs like those in the yard. And cats," he continued, "are to know their place, and not be troublesome."

"There may be truth in what you say," said the Cat calmly; "but I think your view is limited. If you listened, as I do, you would hear men say the world was made for them."

The Cat's Pilgrimage

JAMES ANTHONY FROUDE.

An Encounter

ONE day a friend, who was going away for a few weeks, left his parrot in our care. The bird, homesick and unquiet, climbed to the top of his perch, and rolled his golden eyes warily, wrinkling the white membrane which served for eyelids. My cat, Madame Théophile, had never before seen a parrot, and this strange creature filled her with amazement. Motionless as a cat mummy in its swathing bands, she fixed a profoundly meditative gaze upon the stranger, summoning to her aid all the notions of natural history which she had picked up on the roofs and in the garden. The shadow of her thoughts passed over her changing eyes, and we could read in them the results of her scrutiny: " Decidedly it is a green chicken."

This much ascertained, the cat leaped from the table which she had made her observatory, and crouched low in a corner of the room, flattening herself on the ground, like Gérome's black panther which watches the gazelles coming down to drink from the lake. The parrot followed her movements with feverish anxiety. He ruffled his feathers, shook his chain, raised one claw after another, and whetted his beak on the side of his drinking cup. Instinct told him that here was an enemy plotting mischief. The cat's eyes were all this time fixed upon the bird with terrible intensity, and they said in a language which the poor parrot but too plainly understood: "Green though it be, this chicken is doubtless very good to eat."

We watched the little drama with interest, ready to intervene at need. Madame Théophile crept slowly, almost imperceptibly, forward. Her pink nose quivered, her eyes were half closed, her claws moved in and out of their soft sheaths, little tremors of rapture ran along her spine. She was like an epicure sitting down to a chicken and truffles. Such novel and exotic fare tempted her gluttony.

Suddenly her back bent like a bow, and with a vigorous spring she leaped upon the perch. The parrot, seeing the imminence of his peril, cried in a voice as deep and vibrating as M. Prudhomme's: " Hast thou breakfasted, Jacquot? "

This utterance so terrified the cat that she fell backwards. The blare of a trumpet, the crash of crockery, the report of a pistol could not have made her more dizzy with fright. All her ornithological theories were overthrown.

" And on what? On the king's roast? " continued the parrot.

Then we, the observers, read in the expressive countenance of Madame Théophile: " This is not a bird; it speaks; it is a gentleman."

Ménagerie Intime, THÉOPHILE GAUTIER.

143

The Retired Cat

A poet's cat, sedate and grave
As poet well could wish to have,
Was much addicted to inquire
For nooks to which she might retire,
And where, secure as mouse in chink,
She might repose, or sit and think.
I know not where she caught the trick,—
Nature perhaps herself had cast her
In such a mould *philosophique*,
Or else she learn'd it of her Master.
Sometimes ascending, debonair,
An apple-tree, or lofty pear,
Lodged with convenience in the fork,
She watched the gardener at his work;
Sometimes her ease and solace sought
In an old empty watering-pot;
There wanting nothing save a fan,
To seem some nymph in her sedan,
Apparell'd in exactest sort,
And ready to be borne to Court.

But love of change it seems has place,
Not only in our wiser race;
Cats also feel, as well as we,
That passion's force, and so did she.

Her climbing she began to find
Exposed her too much to the wind,

And the old utensil of tin
Was cold and comfortless within;
She therefore wish'd, instead of those,
Some place of more serene repose,
Where neither cold might come, nor air
Too rudely wanton with her hair;
And sought it in the likeliest mode
Within her Master's snug abode.
    A drawer, it chanced, at bottom lined
With linen of the softest kind,
With such as merchants introduce
From India, for the ladies' use,
A drawer impending o'er the rest,
Half open in the topmost chest,
Of depth enough, and none to spare,
Invited her to slumber there;
Puss with delight beyond expression
Surveyed the scene and took possession.
Recumbent at her ease ere long,
And lull'd by her own humdrum song,
She left the cares of life behind,
And slept as she would sleep her last,
When in came, housewifely inclined,
The chambermaid, and shut it fast,
By no malignity impell'd,
But all unconscious whom it held.

Awaken'd by the shock, cried Puss,
" Was ever cat attended thus!
The open drawer was left, I see,
Merely to prove a nest for me;
For soon as I was well composed,
Then came the maid, and it was closed.
How smooth these kerchiefs and how sweet,
Oh, what a delicate retreat!
I will resign myself to rest,
Till Sol, declining in the west,
Shall call to supper, when, no doubt,
Susan will come and let me out."
    The evening came, the sun descended,
And Puss remain'd still unattended.
The night rolled tardily away
(With her indeed 'twas never day),
The sprightly morn her course renew'd,
The evening grey again ensued,
And Puss came into mind no more
Than if entomb'd the day before.

With hunger pinch'd, and pinch'd for room,
She now presaged approaching doom,
Nor slept a single wink, nor purr'd,
Conscious of jeopardy incurr'd.
    That night by chance, the poet watching,
Heard an inexplicable scratching;
His noble heart went pit-a-pat,
And to himself he said,—" What's that?"

THE CAT

He drew the curtain at his side,
And forth he peep'd, but nothing spied;
Yet, by his ear directed, guess'd
Something imprisoned in the chest,
And, doubtful what, with prudent care
Resolved it should continue there.
At length, a voice which well he knew,
A long and melancholy mew,
Saluting his poetic ears,
Consoled him, and dispelled his fears.
He left his bed, he trod the floor,
He 'gan in haste the drawers explore,
The lowest first, and, without stop,
The rest in order to the top;
For 'tis a truth well known to most,
That whatsoever thing is lost,
We seek it, ere it come to light,
In every cranny but the right.

Forth skipp'd the cat, not now replete
As erst with airy self-conceit,
Nor in her own fond apprehension
A theme for all the world's attention;
But modest, sober, cured of all
Her notions hyperbolical,
And wishing for a place of rest
Anything rather than a chest.
Then stepp'd the poet into bed,
With this reflection in his head.

147

MORAL.

Beware of too sublime a sense
Of your own worth and consequence.
The man who dreams himself so great,
And his importance of such weight,
That all around, in all that's done,
Must move and act for him alone,
Will learn in school of tribulation
The folly of his expectation.

WILLIAM COWPER.

THE CAT ═══════════

A Wanderer

EVERY one is aware that a perfectly comfortable, well-fed cat will occasionally come to his house and settle there, deserting a family by whom it is lamented, and to whom it could, if it chose, find its way back with ease. This conduct is a mystery which may lead us to infer that cats form a great secret society, and that they come and go in pursuance of some policy connected with education, or perhaps with witchcraft. We have known a cat to abandon his home for years. Once in six months he would return, and look about him with an air of some contempt. "Such," he seemed to say, "were my humble beginnings."

ANDREW LANG.

An Outcast

My father had a strong sympathy for cats. This was the result of early experience. He and his brother, knocked pitilessly about in their childhood between the harshness of home and the cruelty of school, had, for solace and alleviation, two well-loved cats. Affection for these animals became a family trait. When we were young, each of us had a kitten. We gathered round the fire at night, and our sleek, well-fed pets sat at our feet, basking in the grateful warmth.

There was one cat, however, that never joined the circle. He was a poor ugly thing, and so conscious of his defects that he held aloof with invincible shyness and reserve. He was the butt, the *souffre douleur* of our little society; and the inborn malignity of our natures found expression in the ridicule with which we pelted him. His name was Moquo. He was thin and weak, his coat was scanty, he needed the warm fireside more than the other cats; but the children frightened him, and his comrades, wrapped snugly in their furry robes, disdained to take any notice of his presence. Only my father would go to the dim, cold corner where he cowered, pick him up, carry him to the hearth, and tuck him safely out of sight under a fold of his own

150

coat. There, warm, safe, and unseen, poor Moquo would take courage, and softly purr his gratitude. Sometimes, however, we caught a glimpse of him, and then, in spite of my father's reproaches, we laughed and jeered at his melancholy aspect. I can still recall the shadowy creature, shrinking away, and seeming to melt into the breast of his protector, closing his eyes as he crept backward, choosing to see and hear nothing.

There came a day when my father left us for a long journey, and all the animals shared our grief at his departure. Time after time his dogs trotted a little way along the road he had taken to Paris, howling piteously for their master. The most desolate creature in the house was Moquo. He trusted no one; but, for a while, would steal to the hearth, looking wistfully and furtively at my father's vacant place. Then, losing hope, he fled to the woods, to resume the wild and wretched life of his infancy; and, though we tried, we never could entice him back to the home where he no longer had a friend.

Mémoires d'une Enfant, ATHANAÏS MICHELET.

A Poet to the Rescue

PASSING yesterday from the greenhouse to the barn, I saw three kittens (for we have so many in our retinue) looking with fixed attention at something which lay coiled up on the threshold of a door. I took but little notice of them at first; but a loud hiss engaged me to attend more closely, when behold — a viper! the largest I remember to have seen, rearing itself, darting its forked tongue, and ejaculating the aforementioned hiss at the nose of a kitten, almost in contact with its lips. I ran into the hall for a hoe with a long handle, with which I intended to assail him, and, returning in a few seconds, missed him: he was gone, and I feared had escaped me. Still, however, the kittens sat watching immovably upon the same spot. I concluded therefore that, sliding between the door and the threshold, he had found his way out of the garden into the yard. I went round immediately, and there found him in close conversation with the old cat, whose curiosity, being excited by so novel an appearance, inclined her to pat his head repeatedly with her fore foot,— with her claws, however, sheathed, and not in anger, but in the way of philosophical inquiry and examination. To prevent her falling a victim to so laudable an exercise of her talents, I interposed in a moment with the hoe, and performed upon him an act of decapitation, which, though not immediately mortal, proved so in the end.

WILLIAM COWPER *to the Rev. W. Unwin.*

The Colubriad

Close by the threshold of a door nail'd fast
Three kittens sat; each kitten looked aghast.
I, passing swift and inattentive by,
At the three kittens cast a careless eye;
Not much concerned to know what they did there,
Nor deeming kittens worth a poet's care.
But presently a loud and furious hiss
Caus'd me to stop, and to exclaim, " What's this? "
When lo! upon the threshold met my view,
With head erect, and eyes of fiery hue,
A viper, long as Count de Grasse's queue.
Forth from his head his forked tongue he throws,
Darting it full against a kitten's nose;
Who, never having seen in field or house
The like, sat still and silent as a mouse;
Only projecting, with attention due,
Her whisker'd face, she asked him, " Who are you? "
On to the hall I went, with pace not slow,
But swift as lightning, for a long Dutch hoe:
With which well arm'd, I hastened to the spot,
To find the viper,— but I saw him not.
And, turning up the leaves and shrubs around,
Found only that he was not to be found.
But still the kittens, sitting as before,
Sat watching close the bottom of the door.
" I hope," said I, " the villain I would kill
Has slipt between the door and the door-sill,

THE CAT

And if I make despatch and follow hard,
No doubt but I shall find him in the yard."
For long ere now it should have been rehears'd,
'Twas in the garden that I saw him first.
E'en there I found him, there the full-grown cat
His head, with velvet paw, did gently pat,
As curious as the kittens erst had been
To learn what this phenomenon might mean.
Fill'd with heroic ardour at the sight,
And fearing every moment he might bite,
And rob our household of our only cat
That was of age to combat with a rat,
With outstretch'd hoe I slew him at the door,
And taught him never to come there no more.

WILLIAM COWPER.

Discipline

A FEMALE cat is kept young in spirit and supple in body by the restless vivacity of her kittens. She plays with her little ones, fondles them, pursues them if they roam too far, and corrects them sharply for all the faults to which feline infancy is heir. A kitten dislikes being washed quite as much as a child does, especially in the neighbourhood of its ears. It tries to escape the infliction, rolls away, paddles with its little paws, and behaves as naughtily as it knows how, until a smart slap brings it suddenly back to subjection. Pussy has no confidence in moral suasion, but implicitly follows Solomon's somewhat neglected advice. I was once told a pleasant story of an English cat who had reared several large families, and who, dozing one day before the nursery fire, was disturbed and annoyed by the whining of a fretful child. She bore it as long as she could, waiting for the nurse to interpose her authority; then, finding passive endurance had outstripped the limits of her patience, she arose, crossed the room, jumped on the sofa, and twice with her strong soft paw, which had chastised many an erring kitten, deliberately boxed the little girl's ears,— after which she returned to her slumbers.

The Fireside Sphinx, AGNES REPPLIER.

A Letter of Condolence

As one ought to be particularly careful to avoid blunders in a compliment of condolence, it would be a sensible satisfaction to me (before I testify my sorrow, and the sincere part I take in your misfortune) to know for certain who it is I lament. I knew Zara and Selima (Selima was it, or Fatima?), or rather I knew them both together; for I cannot justly say which was which. Then as to your handsome Cat, the name you distinguish her by, I am no less at a loss, as well knowing one's handsome cat is always the cat one likes best; or if one be alive and the other dead, it is usually the latter that is the handsomest. Besides, if the point were never so clear, I hope you do not think me so ill-bred or so imprudent as to forfeit all my interest in the survivor. Oh, no! I would rather seem to mistake, and imagine to be sure it must be the tabby one that has met with this sad accident. . . . I feel (as you have done long since) that I have very little to say, at least in prose. Somebody will be the better for it; I do not mean you, but your Cat, *feue* Mademoiselle Sélime, whom I am about to immortalize for one week or fortnight.

THOMAS GRAY *to Horace Walpole.*

157

On the Death of a Favourite Cat, Drowned in a Tub of Gold-Fishes

'Twas on a lofty vase's side,
Where China's gayest art had dyed
  The azure flowers that blow,
Demurest of the tabby kind,
The pensive Selima, reclined,
  Gazed on the lake below.

Her conscious tail her joy declared;
The fair round face, the snowy beard,
  The velvet of her paws,
Her coat that with the tortoise vies,
Her ears of jet and emerald eyes,
  She saw, and purred applause.

Still had she gazed, but 'midst the tide
Two angel forms were seen to glide,—
  The Genii of the stream:
Their scaly armour's Tyrian hue,
Through richest purple, to the view
  Betrayed a golden gleam.

The hapless nymph with wonder saw:
A whisker first, and then a claw,
  With many an ardent wish,
She stretched in vain to reach the prize;
What female heart can gold despise?
  What cat's averse to fish?

THE CAT

Presumptuous maid! with looks intent,
Again she stretched, again she bent,
  Nor knew the gulf between.
Malignant Fate sat by and smiled,
The slippery verge her feet beguiled,
  She stumbled headlong in.

Eight times emerging from the flood,
She mewed to every watery god
  Some speedy aid to send.
No Dolphin came, no Nereid stirred,
Nor cruel Tom nor Susan heard;
  A favourite has no friend!

From hence, ye Beauties! undeceived,
Know one false step is ne'er retrieved,
  And be with caution bold:
Not all that tempts your wandering eyes
And heedless hearts is lawful prize,
  Nor all that glisters, gold.

THOMAS GRAY.

The Cat in the Nursery.

Pussy sat beside the fire
Pussy was so fair,
In came a little dog
Pussy are you there?

Education

When People think that Kittens play,
  It's really quite the other way;
For when they chase the Ball or Bobbin,
  They learn to catch a Mouse or Robin.

The Kitten, deaf to Duty's call,
 Who will not chase the bounding Ball,
A hungry Cathood will enjoy,
  The scorn of Mouse, and Bird, and Boy.

OLIVER HERFORD.

Marigold

She moved through the garden in glory, because
She had very long claws at the end of her paws.
Her back was arched, her tail was high,
A green fire glared in her vivid eye;
And all the Toms, though never so bold,
Quailed at the martial Marigold.

RICHARD GARNETT.

THE CAT

" Pussy-cat, Pussy-cat,
   Where have you been? "
" I've been to London,
   To look at the Queen."
" Pussy-cat, Pussy-cat,
   What did you do there? "
" I frightened a little mouse
   Under her chair."

There was a wee bit mousikie,
   That lived in Gilberaty, O;
It couldna get a bite o' cheese,
   For cheety-poussie-catty, O.

It said unto the cheesikie,
   " Oh, fain wad I be at ye, O,
If it were na for the cruel paws
   O' cheety-poussie-catty, O."

Nursery Rhymes.

A Sea Fight

"PRINCE," said the White Cat, "let us be merry. I have ordered a naval combat between my cats and the terrible rats of this country. My cats will perhaps be a little embarrassed because they fear the water; but otherwise they would have had too much the advantage, and one should equalise matters as far as one is able."

The Prince admired the wisdom of the Cat, and went with her to a terrace overlooking the sea and the assembled fleets. The ships in which the cats embarked were made of pieces of cork, and sailed buoyantly over the waves. The rats had joined together a number of egg-shells, and into these their sailors bravely climbed. The battle was hard fought. The rats never hesitated to fling themselves into the water, and, because they swam so well, they were many times on the point of victory. But Minagrobis, admiral of the feline fleet, saved it from disaster. He attacked and promptly devoured the enemy's great captain, a wise and experienced old rat, who had been three times around the world, and whose death filled his followers with despair.

The White Cat would not, however, permit the destruction of the enemy. She was a sagacious ruler, and she knew that if there were no more rats and mice left in the land, her subjects would live in idleness, which is a dangerous thing, and might make them disobedient and rebellious.

La Chatte Blanche,

MARIE DE BERNEVILLE (Comtesse d'Aulnoy).

Six little mice sat down to spin,
Pussy passed by, and she peeped in.
" What are you at, my little men? "
" Making coats for gentlemen."
" Shall I come in and bite off your threads? "
" No, no, Miss Pussy, you'll bite off our heads."

Pussycat, wussycat, with a white foot,
When is your wedding, and I'll come to't?
The beer's to brew, the bread's to bake,
Pussycat, wussycat, don't be late.

Nursery Rhymes.

Mère Michel

Mère Michel is calling, calling, from her window
  high,
"My pussy cat is lost or stolen; find him, passers-by."
Papa Lustucru is walking, walking far below;
"Your pussy cat was never lost, and this is all I
  know."

Mère Michel is weeping, weeping, by her window
  pane;
"Papa Lustucru, I pray you bring him home again."
Papa Lustucru is shaking, shaking hard his head;
"You must give a recompense;" and this is all he said.

Mère Michel is smiling, smiling;—"You shall have a
  kiss.
Bring me back my pussy cat, and I'll not grudge you
  this."
Papa Lustucru is hastening, hastening fast away;
"Your cat was for a rabbit sold, and this is market
  day."

French Nursery Rhyme.

The Cattie Sits in the Kiln-Ring

The cattie sits in the kiln-ring,
　　Spinning, spinning;
And by cam a little wee mousie,
　　Rinning, rinning.

" Oh, what's that you're spinning, my loesome,
　Loesome lady? "
" I'm spinning a sark to my young son,"
　Said she, said she.

" Weel mot he brook it, my loesome,
　Loesome lady."
" Gin he dinna brook it weel, he may brook it ill,"
　Said she, said she.

" I soopit my house, my loesome,
　Loesome lady."
" 'Twas a sign ye didna sit amang dirt then,"
　Said she, said she.

" I fand twall pennies, my winsome,
　Winsome lady."
" 'Twas a sign ye warna sillerless,"
　Said she, said she.

" I gaed to the market, my loesome,
　Loesome lady."
" 'Twas a sign ye didna sit at hame then,"
　Said she, said she.

THE CAT

" I coft a sheepie's head, my winsome,
  Winsome lady."
" 'Twas a sign ye warna kitchenless,"
  Said she, said she.

" I put it in my pottie to boil, my loesome,
  Loesome lady."
" 'Twas a sign ye didna eat it raw,"
  Said she, said she.

" I put in my winnock to cool, my winsome,
  Winsome lady."
" 'Twas a sign ye didna burn your chafts then,"
  Said she, said she.

" By cam a cattie, and ate it a' up, my loesome,
  Loesome lady."
" And sae will I you,— worrie, worrie, gnash, gnash,"
  Said she, said she.

                    Scotch Nursery Rhyme.

Grisette Dines

Always well behaved am I,
Never scratch and never cry;
Only touch the diner's hand,
So that he can understand
That I want a modest share
Of the good things that are there.
If he pay but scanty heed
To my little stomach's need,
I beg him with a mew polite
To give me just a single bite.
Greedy though that diner be,
He will share his meal with me.

From the French of MME. DESHOULLIÈRES.

THE END

INDEX OF AUTHORS

www.ingramcontent.com/pod-product-compliance
Lightning Source LLC
Chambersburg PA
CBHW021231090426
42740CB00006B/477